# ROAD TO EXCELLENCE

# Incredible
# 5S
## for
# Productivity Improvement

## Upali Marasinghe
### (BSc, MPA, LLB, Attorney at Law)

Copyright © 2012 Upali Marasinghe
First Edition – November 2012

**ISBN**
978-1-4602-0747-5 (Paperback)
978-1-4602-0748-2 (eBook)

All rights reserved.

No part of this publication may be reproduced in any form, or by any means, electronic or mechanical, including photocopying, recording, or any information browsing, storage, or retrieval system, without permission in writing from the publisher.

Published by:

## FriesenPress

Suite 300 – 852 Fort Street
Victoria, BC, Canada V8W 1H8

www.friesenpress.com

Distributed to the trade by The Ingram Book Company

# Table of Contents

From the author ............................................................. vii
Preface ............................................................................ x
About this book .......................................................... xiii
Introduction .................................................................. 1
Chapter 1 ....................................................................... 4
    *Productivity*
Chapter 2 ..................................................................... 22
    *Efficiency and Effectiveness*
Chapter 3 ..................................................................... 25
    *Productivity Comparison of some Countries*
Chapter 4 ..................................................................... 57
    *Myths about Productivity*
Chapter 5 ..................................................................... 66
    *Benefits of Productivity Improvement*
Chapter 6 ..................................................................... 76
    *Sectors of Productivity*
Chapter 7 ..................................................................... 79
    *Areas to be focused on in Productivity Improvement*
Chapter 8 ..................................................................... 90
    *Various Methodologies to be used to improve Productivity*
Chapter 9 ................................................................... 115
    *5S Concept*

# Table of Contents

Chapter 10 .................................................... 124
    *Seiri-Sorting and Organization*

Chapter 11 .................................................... 130
    *Seiton- Arranging and Neatness - (Set in Order)*

Chapter 12 .................................................... 149
    *Seiso – Cleaning / Shining*

Chapter 13 .................................................... 154
    *Seiketsu – Standardization*

Chapter 14 .................................................... 169
    *Shitshuke- Sustaining/Discipline*

Chapter 15 .................................................... 173
    *Challenges for Implementation of 5S*

Chapter 16 .................................................... 181
    *Application of 5S Concept to your Mind*

*Make Your*

*Lifestyle*

*Productive*

Other publications of the author

- Quality Circles & QC tools for Productivity Improvement
- 5S for Productivity Improvement
- GCE A/L Chemistry – Resources
- GCE A/L Chemistry – Kinetics
- GCE A/L Chemistry - Isomerism
- GCE A/L Chemistry – Mole
- GCE A/L Chemistry - Industrial Chemistry
- GCE O/L Science (Q & A) I
- GCE O/L Science (Q & A) II
- Science for Children

# FROM THE AUTHOR

The prosperity and development of a country depend on the contribution made to the economy by its citizens. It is a prime responsibility of every citizen to contribute to build the nation and enrich its sound economic development. Consider the case of Japan. After the Second World War, which ended in 1945, the Japanese community inherited a devastated country, destroyed buildings, etc., and these factors led to very poor economic conditions. However, the need to rebuild the nation and to have a well-committed community was obvious and this message of individual responsibility in the rebuilding was delivered to every sector in Japan gradually until there was complete penetration. During the past six decades, Japan had targets in every sector, such as education, economy and industry. As a result of this commitment and clear policies formulated by the Japanese government, the per capita gross domestic product has escalated and it is around USD 42,830 (year 2010). What does it mean? It means one Japanese citizen is producing goods and services worth USD

42,830 per year. Most developing countries are very far from this figure.

At present, not only Japan, but also Singapore, Malaysia and Korea, have succeeded in uplifting their economy and they are now on a competitive level with other developed countries in the world. The reasons behind this success are dedication, commitment, clear economic policies and good governance. Each policy decision has been taken for the sake of the public. The private sector as well as the public sector in these developed countries has been able to manage their resources optimally and focus on customer satisfaction. This kind of achievement is not an easy task. So what is the main secret behind this? The secret is the implementation of productivity concepts.

Disseminating the message of productivity to every citizen and motivating them to act accordingly is a fruitful way to achieve higher productivity levels. Japan was able to implement these productivity concepts quickly by introducing them to the public sector, private sector, schools and at the community level. The final outcome of this effort was implanting productivity concepts as built-in tools in the daily life of Japanese citizens. Hence, currently the Japanese community follows so many productive strategies. Japan has a dedicated, devoted and motivated work force/community and as a result, Japan is running fast towards a sound economy even though there are slight fluctuations. In addition, Japan always updates knowledge and disseminates it very quickly and is always investigating new strategies. Nowadays this methodology has been adopted by several countries such as Singapore, Malaysia and Korea. However, in developing countries, it is hard to see us applying productivity concepts on a vast scale although a small number of organizations have started and gained impressive results.

Small scale implementation of these concepts does not count for a big percentage of economic development. Even though a number of organizations have implemented these concepts in their organizations, it is not adequate to make a substantial positive impact on a mass scale like it was done in Japan, Singapore and Korea. If this strategy is adopted, any country will be able to progress rapidly as well.

Upali Marasinghe
Toronto ON
Canada
upalima2002@yahoo.co.uk

# PREFACE

There is a statement that "Productivity is everybody's business". It means that everybody has a specific role and responsibility to contribute to improve productivity. The accumulated effort of all citizens makes a country more productive. However, poor communication of the message on productivity has kept out most of the citizens from the productivity improvement drive.

Most of the under-developed and developing countries face this problem because of lack of a strong mechanism to take this message to the grass roots level. A lack of resources also acts as a strong impeding factor for this. However, the rate of income generation of a country depends on the productivity level. So everybody should try to improve the wealth of their own country and then such countries can face challenges more easily.

In order to disseminate the productivity message, different long-term and short-term measures can be taken. Developed countries in the Asian region such as Japan, Singapore, Malaysia and Korea, followed different means to disseminate this message to every sector in their countries. This message was also taken to the school level and they were able to make a substantial attitude change. As a result, they were able to form a productive workforce. Among the strategies which were taken to disseminate the productivity message, books, leaflets, teledramas, films, demonstrations and models played a significant role in these developed countries.

When I worked in the District Office of Agrarian services, Chilaw, Sri Lanka, in the 1990s, I was able to read a short article on productivity improvement. At the end of the article, it gave emphasis on the implementation of 5S as an initial start to the productivity improvement journey.

A curiosity was born in my mind and I was compelled to find out what the 5S was. I went through different sources including the Internet, and I was able to collect a little knowledge on productivity concepts and 5S. Then, I applied these concepts to my office and, now I feel that it was a very small effort. However, I was able to make a significant change in the office system, response time, and office environment as well as behavioural patterns of the public servants in the office.

These positive achievements pushed me to seek further knowledge on productivity improvement concepts and methods. I was able to gather more information on productivity. As a result, I conducted more lectures and seminars for public offices. Later, I was able to apply these concepts to different departments which in I worked.

These changes made me more courageous and I delivered many lectures on productivity. Meanwhile, I felt compelled to write a few articles and some small books on productivity in Sinhala Medium (one of the official language in Sri Lanka). A simple thought came to my mind to write a series of articles on productivity in order to broaden my effort in disseminating the productivity message. However, it was converted to writing a book because of the encouragement and assistance given by Mrs. Jayne Long, an instructor of a course called **Communication Skills for Professionals** which I followed in Canada. Finally the task of editing of the book was also undertaken by Jayne voluntarily and it was a great advantage I had.

Hence, my sincere gratitude and thanks to Jayne. Before concluding my remarks, I thank all my friends who assisted me to make these achievements. I also cannot forget the assistance given by Mr. Ashoka Perera, Productivity Development Assistant of office in typesetting of the book. My Sincere thanks to Miss Sadisi Mallawaarachchi for assisting me on proof reading. Finally, I sincerely hope that this book will make others aware of productivity concepts and encourage them to align their lifestyle more productively.

**Upali Marasinghe**

# ABOUT THIS BOOK

**Upali Marasinghe** clearly has one thing on his mind: to see a more prosperous and peaceful society. This book presents a blueprint for economic advancement at an international, national, workplace, community, family or individual level. He explains the theories of productivity clearly, comprehensively, yet in simple language, providing both conceptual information and practical examples. The methodology to increase productivity is outlined, step by step.

By studying the contents of this book and putting into practice its guidance, all levels of society could achieve greater productivity leading to increased prosperity. Individual citizens, in their daily lives, could take advantage of its insight; small and large businesses could improve their results; and governments at the local and national levels could advance the well-being of the nation.

In preparing this book, Upali is modelling the very theme of his book – that every individual has the responsibility and immense capacity to make their world a better place.

Jayne Long, Instructor
MicroSkills Community Development Centre
Toronto, Canada.

# INTRODUCTION

The 5S concept, which is the initial step to productivity improvement, originated in Japan. Even before the introduction of this concept in Japan, most of the people around the world practised some steps in their day-to-day life. However, it became popularized as a tool of productivity improvement after it was implemented in Japan.

After the Second World War, Japan stepped up to a rapid industrial development and most organizations, including companies, factories, schools and public sector organizations, followed management principles especially targeted on high productivity and quality. Teamwork, appropriate management techniques, participatory approaches and leadership skills were the main key elements behind this success and the 5S concept was used as a facilitator and a catalyst in order to run organizations smoothly. Even today, Japanese treat the 5S concept as a foundation of productivity and quality improvement.

There seem to be fewer labour disputes in organizations which introduced the 5S concept. In fact, perhaps zero disputes can be observed. Trade union activities, such as strikes and work to rule, have not been observed.

In addition, all equipment is maintained properly with no breakdowns and no defective instruments. As a result, rejected items are minimal. In order to have such an efficient system, the 5S concept has been conveyed to every worker and employee in all organizations.

Having observed the results of this system implemented in Japan, countries such as Singapore, Korea, Malaysia and Taiwan have been compelled to introduce the 5S concept in their countries, and they have also gained excellent results. After introducing the 5S concept in Japan, it was possible to get new ideas and suggestions which led to a high level of productivity. Linkages between top, middle and lower level employees were strengthened. A dedicated workforce contributed to the development and creation of sustainable organizations. Hence, the top management felt much easier about administering their organizations. As a main outcome of this, management was able to minimize resources and efforts to achieve expected levels.

The 5S concept which was a good tool at the workplace gradually trickled down to the household level. Thus, this concept became a day-to-day practice and was bound tightly with the routines of life. As a result, every citizen was able to contribute to the gross domestic product in Japan directly or indirectly. That led to high economic development in Japan.

A very important feature of the 5S concept is that it can be introduced anywhere, to any community, or any organization, despite race, religion etc. However, before going into the 5S concept in detail, it is very important to understand the concept of productivity because 5S is also one component of productivity improvement.

In western countries also, this concept has been practiced and remarkable results have been gained. This practice is commonly called "Housekeeping" in western countries. However, whether it is called 5S or housekeeping, the same methodology is practiced. Hence, this concept is accepted worldwide as it gives tangible outcomes in every sector.

# CHAPTER 1

## Productivity

The word "Productivity" can be simply explained as the ratio between inputs and outputs.

$$\text{Productivity} = \frac{\text{Value of the outputs}}{\text{Value of the inputs}}$$

For example, if USD 10,000 is spent and USD 12,000 is earned, the productivity of that transaction can be written as 12,000/10,000 = 1.2

Let's study the following two situations. Using the amount spent and earned by A and B with two separate transactions, try to calculate productivity.

$$A \rightarrow \quad \frac{\text{Output}}{\text{Input}} = \frac{12{,}000}{10{,}000} = 1.2$$

So the productivity of A is 1.2.

$$B \rightarrow \quad \frac{\text{Output}}{\text{Input}} = \frac{18{,}000}{15{,}000} = 1.2$$

So the productivity of B is also 1.2.

According to the above calculation, the productivity of both A and B is 1.2. However, the amount each has spent is different. The amount each has earned is also different. Their profits are also different. A's profit is USD 2,000 and B's profit is USD 3,000. According to the profit calculation, B is better than A because B has earned USD 3,000 as profit. However, the productivity ratios of A and B are the same. The reason for this is that the productivity is calculated by finding the ratio between inputs and outputs of A and B.

What does this mean? It means the productivity is not the profit. In order to measure the productivity, profit is not the only factor. Hence, it is not realistic to say that profitable organizations are always productive. Perhaps the productivity of a person or an organization with less profit may be higher than that of a person or an organization with higher profit. Therefore, it is very important to be careful when productivity is calculated. The financial achievement alone does not determine whether that organization is productive or not. Therefore, now it is clear that all inputs and all outputs should be used to calculate productivity.

What is input? What is output? Inputs include money, raw materials, time, labour, machines which are used and output is what we get as the end product. When output is considered, physical output, social output and cultural output should also be taken into consideration.

For example, we can examine the productivity of building a tank or a reservoir by farmers for an agricultural purpose. The inputs of this event are money and the value of labour given by the farmers and other workers as well as the cost of materials and machines and tools. The outputs of this activity after a tank or reservoir are finished, the amount of water stored in it and the improved harvest which results from it. These are direct outputs. In addition to the direct outputs, there are some indirect outputs such as the ability to use the water for animal husbandry and the environmental benefits. Thus, direct outputs and indirect outputs should be taken into consideration when productivity is calculated.

The productivity measured, taking all inputs and all outputs, is called "Total Factor Productivity." However, it is difficult to calculate intangible outputs when Total Factor Productivity is measured. Thus, it is advisable to use all outputs which are computable. Even though we cannot calculate intangible or indirect outputs, these things should be taken into consideration as well as direct or tangible outputs.

Such calculations are very important when the feasibility of a project is evaluated. For instance, consider the impact of investing in education. By investing money in education, a country will have an educated generation which contributes vitally to the economic development of that country. Furthermore it will become an asset to the country and it is the direct impact of investing money. In addition to the educated generation, the country will have a more civilized society as a result of investing money in education and this is an indirect impact. A civilized and educated society leads to reduced crime. It minimizes the cost of maintenance of the prisons and judicial system. So the government will be able to save money and divert it into investment in fruitful development schemes. Thus, spending money on maintenance of prisons is less productive than in investing the same amount of money in educational development.

Productivity improvement is everybody's business. Everybody including both managerial level and operational level staff should contribute to productivity improvement in their own organizations. Everybody should know about productivity and how to improve it. As we know, inputs and outputs are the key points which we have to take into consideration when the productivity is improved and measured.

There are five major ways to improve the productivity ratio. These are:

1. Minimizing inputs while outputs are kept constant
2. Maximizing outputs while inputs are kept constant
3. Minimizing inputs and maximizing outputs
4. Increasing inputs a little amount and trying to get a large increase in output
5. Decreasing inputs by a large amount and maintaining output at a constant level

Of the above-mentioned five ways, the first three are the most important and common methods. The other two methods are used occasionally and when only the first three steps are not feasible.

Let us consider a few examples of how to apply the above first three methods to improve productivity.

Traffic control is one of the important duties of police departments in most developing countries. We can apply the above-mentioned principles to this activity in order to improve the productivity level of this task. Suppose about 1,000 police officers are engaged every morning to control traffic in the city. If this activity is performed productively, the time taken for a vehicle to get to point B from point A should be minimized.

Let us assume a vehicle takes 60 minutes to reach point B from point A under the current situation. This is a result of the collective effort of 1,000 police officers. So the number of police officers is the input and the time taken to reach B to A is the output.

If the number of police officers is kept constant and the time taken to reach B from A can be reduced to 45 minutes, the productivity goes up. In order to do that all police officers can be trained well and compelled to perform their duties in a more organized manner. This is one way of improving productivity. As a result of this, passengers can reach their destinations within a shorter time period than they did earlier. So the training given to police officers is also accumulated to inputs.

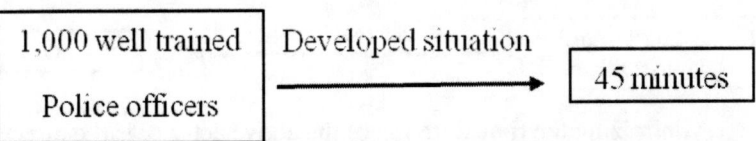

The second method is to keep the output, i.e., the time of 60 minutes, constant and minimize the inputs. As mentioned above, police officers can be trained and the number of police officers can be brought down to 750 and still maintain the time taken to reach B from A at 60 minutes. Now the number of police officers has been reduced although the time has not been reduced. Reducing the number of police officers means reducing resources. Hence, this is another way of improving productivity. Although the productivity is increased by this method, the customers or people who use the road don't feel the positive impact. Hence, the first method is better than the second method.

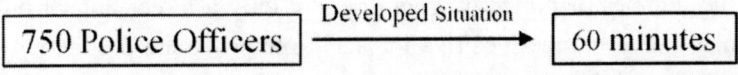

However, the best method is the third one. That is minimizing inputs and outputs. As explained earlier, police officers can be trained well and the number of police officers assigned to the same job can be reduced to 750. Meanwhile they can be instructed to maintain the system well and the time taken to reach from A to B can be reduced to 45 minutes. Then the number of police officers is reduced and the time is also reduced. So the output or results will be improved more than the above-mentioned methods 1 & 2.

```
┌─────────────────┐      Productive Situation     ┌────────────┐
│ 750 well trained│ ────────────────────────────▶ │ 45 minutes │
│ Police Officers │                                └────────────┘
└─────────────────┘
```

Minimizing the time duration of the above activity is the direct impact of this task. If this activity is performed well, there are also many indirect positive results which contribute to the productivity improvement of this activity. By minimizing the time taken to reach B from point A, all road users can reduce the time spent on traveling. They can use the time saved for another useful activity. Imagine how much fuel can be saved daily by reducing the travelling time by 15 minutes. It is a remarkable saving and positive impact to the country's economy. In addition, by reducing the number of police officers by 250, the police department can save money and minimize administrative costs. Such police officers can be diverted to other important tasks. It is clearly understood that reducing the time taken for this task and reducing the number of police officers give not only a direct impact but also many indirect positive impacts to improve the productivity of this activity.

Another activity that we can consider is the train system operated by the Railway Department. Imagine that the number of trains operated daily is 150 and the number of employees of the railway department who operate these 150 trains is 10,000. In addition, consider the average speed of trains as 50 km/h. In order to operate the railway system successfully, the commitment and dedication of every employee, including drivers, guards, maintenance crews, etc, is essential. By managing inputs and outputs properly, the Railway Department can also improve productivity.

Keeping the number of employees as it is and maximizing the service is one way of improving productivity. In order to do that, all employees should be trained well to develop their skills and attitudes. Then, all the trains can be operated in a timely fashion and the number of trains can be increased.

The alternate way to improve the productivity of the train service is reducing staff to 7,500 and operating the system without any new improvement. That is minimizing inputs while keeping the output constant. However, as we mentioned in the example of the police department, the passengers do not feel the impact of this step.

The best way to improve the productivity in the railway system is reducing the number of employees to 7,500 while increasing the number of trains operated and increasing the speed of the trains. This can be done by improved human resource management. Introducing new knowledge, skills and attitudes to employees is the best way of encouraging employees to reach maximum output levels. In order to maximize service efficiency, many new developments can be introduced. Some of them are installing automatic ticket machines, a computerized control system, modern engines, etc, as well as incentive schemes for employees who perform well. This kind of system minimizes the operational costs and maximizes the service rendered to the general public. It is the direct impact of a productive railway system. Indirectly, passengers can go to their workplaces and destinations on time, delays can be minimized and they will be happy about the service.

As discussed above, every organization and every person can improve productivity by managing inputs and outputs properly. However, in order to achieve the maximum level of productivity, the above-explained strategies are not adequate. In addition to those strategies, there are three main principles which have to be fulfilled. Whether it is a product or a service, these three principles should be applied.

1. Improving the quality of the product or service
2. Promoting the product or the service in the market
3. Adding value to the product or service

## 1. Improving the quality of the products or service

### 1.1. Improving the quality of a product

Products are tangible. So the quality of a product can be improved easily. For example, consider a kind of soap. The main purpose of soap is its ability to remove dirty particles. Even though the soap removes dirt very well, the customers are not always compelled to buy it because the customers are very concerned about other features of the soap. If the soap causes itching, customers do not buy it although such soap washes well. Therefore, the producers should think of these facts in order to have a good market share for their product. In addition to the washing ability the producer has to add fragrance, attractive colours and it should be sent to the market with attractive packaging. All these factors contribute to the improvement of quality of this product. Such products can be priced a little bit higher than lower quality products. Hence, it definitely contributes to the productivity improvement of the company.

Consider another example. The production of high quality notebooks (exercise books) leads to higher levels of productivity of that business.

In order to improve the quality of notebooks, good paper with standard thickness (gsm) should be used. Such paper should not be blotted. Further, the rules should be printed clearly and with equal spaces. In addition the cover page should be printed in an attractive manner. So the final finishing of the book should be of high quality. Customers always tend to buy such products and the producer will not face any difficulty in selling such items because of its high quality.

## 1.2. Improving the quality of a service

Unlike products, quality improvement of a service is more difficult because service quality is intangible and the customers feel it at the time they receive the service. In order to provide good service, the staff of the organization should be trained and they should be prepared for it, even emotionally. However, improving quality of a service can be done and it is achievable.

When you go to the bank to deposit or withdraw money, what type of service do you get from the staff? Your ultimate objective is to deposit or withdraw money. The staff of the bank can provide this service satisfactorily or unsatisfactorily. It depends on the systems installed in the bank, the commitment of the employees, etc.

In order to improve the quality of their service, they can minimize the waiting time. They can provide some seating arrangements for customers and attractive reading materials about the bank services. The whole environment can be developed in a pleasant manner. All forms can be filled by the counter person on behalf of the customer. Steps which can be taken to improve the quality of service depend on creativity. ATMs, web banking and telephone banking facilities are some of the improved methods to enhance the quality and productivity. Therefore, different measures can be taken to enhance the quality of the service.

*Pleasant Environment*

*Unpleasant Environments*

Public service also comes under the service category. Hence, productivity improvement methods can also be applied to the public sector institutions and service quality can be improved.

When a public servant retires, he is entitled to a commuted pension. That has to be paid at the time of retirement. About 20 years ago, this commuted pension was paid normally after a long period but presently there are some developments in the system to expedite this payment. However, no one can say that is 100% perfect. Hence, the quality of this service can also be improved further. That means if this commuted pension can be paid on the day he retires, it is the best way to perform this activity. Then the pensioner will also be happy and the service will also be satisfactory. The main point of this is the time taken to prepare his document and issue the cheque is the same even it is delayed months and months. By delaying it, the only thing the public sector gets is criticism and a bad reputation. By having the same effort and same cost, the public servants can perform their duties quickly and in a quality manner. If a cheque is delayed, the customer is also dissatisfied. If a cheque is issued promptly, the customer is satisfied. The response of a satisfied customer and dissatisfied customer is totally different. As far as productivity is concerned, customer satisfaction is the prime objective. Therefore, it is understood that every system should be aligned to customer satisfaction.

The Department of Highways is another organization which provides services to the public. When roads are maintained, quality should be maintained properly. However, on many occasions it is hard to observe quality maintenance. In order to fill the pits and damage on the roads, a tar mixture is used. The way of doing this is to put down some mixture and compact it with a compactor. If the compacting is not done properly, there are some bumps on the road. This kind of task completion is not correct and the quality is also poor. In addition, if compacting is not done properly, the durability of this filling is in question. Within a shorter period it may be removed very easily and another refill has to be done.

Imagine the cost of filling an area of one square feet is USD 10. If refilling has to be done regularly, the cost would be doubled or tripled. If the refilling is done properly that task can be completed by spending USD10 only and it lasts a long period. It is worth spending USD 12 to do it properly rather than doing it at a lower cost again and again because the cumulative cost would be very high.

*Poor quality road refilling*

In developed countries, low quality tasks with lower cost are not encouraged. Even with slightly higher costs, high quality tasks are encouraged because the durability of such tasks is higher than low quality tasks.

In developed countries such as the USA, Canada, the UK, France, Japan, Singapore, and Malaysia, when pits/ potholes on the roads are filled, it is done properly. First, the edges of the pits are cut in order to have a fresh surface. Later all debris including dust is removed and then the mixture is applied to the pit and compacted well using strong compactors. Finally, the surface is finished well in order to avoid any bumps. The procedure is a little bit costly but it is long-lasting. So there is no necessity to repair it frequently. This indicates that any task should be performed with high quality although the cost is higher. It is worth more than doing poor quality work with lower costs. In order to achieve higher productivity levels, high quality should be maintained.

## 2. Promoting the product or the service in the market

Another important step to improve productivity is promoting the product or service in the market. As far as a product is concerned, promotion is easier. Attractive advertising can be used to convince the customers. In addition, famous characters / celebrities such as singers or actors can be used to promote the product. For example, famous actresses praise the quality of products through different media and then the customers are tempted to buy such items.

A service can also be promoted. Public organizations as well as other private service organizations can deliver messages to the public explaining their quality service. Some organizations have created some promotional statements. One public organization has created a statement as **"We assure the payment of commuted pension on the day of retirement."** This kind of statement enhances the image of the organization among the public. One mobile telecom company used "wireless - worriless communication" as their promotional motto. A world famous cricket team wears T- shirts with a brand name of tea when they play. Some organizations have publicized or even guaranteed the waiting time. So it is a very good indicator to customers how long they have to wait to get the job done.

I recall on the day students, including myself, were admitted to the advanced level classes. The principal of the school used a statement to promote the school at the time he addressed all the parents. The statement is: **"I cannot ensure that all students will be able to enter the university. But I can ensure that every student in the school will be a fruitful person to the society."** By using such kinds of statements, every organization can promote its product or service.

## 3. Adding value to the product or service

In order to improve the productivity of a product or a service, value addition is another important step. By adding value, the customers will be more satisfied. When a product is developed step by step, its value automatically goes up. For example, the paddy harvested from the fields has a specific denomination or value. If this paddy is converted to rice, the denomination of the rice is higher than the value of the paddy used to produce rice. By converting paddy into rice, the value is added to the product. If the same amount of rice is converted to rice flour, its value is higher than the amount of rice. Likewise the rice flour can also be converted to different products. By continuing this process, value is added to the product gradually. The ultimate result would be high income. High income leads to high productivity levels.

*Value Addition*    *Value Addition*    *Value Addition*

Paddy ⟶ Rice ⟶ Rice floor ⟶ Biscuits

A bottle of soft drink can be sold without chilling at a lower price. If it is chilled, it can be sold at a higher price. This is also a value addition to the bottle of soft drink.

Vegetables harvested on a farm can be sent to the market with soil on them. It definitely gives less return. If these vegetables are washed and cleaned well and segregated according to the sizes, the value or denomination of such vegetables is higher than the soiled vegetables. In order to add further value to the cleaned vegetables, they can be packed well and sent to the market. By following this procedure, the producer can get more income which means higher productivity.

As explained above, the producer benefits from value addition. However, the value addition concept can be explained from the point of view of the customer. If the customer gets more value for what he pays, that can also be treated as value addition from the point of view of the customer.

When a notebook (exercise book) is purchased by a customer, his main intention is to use that book for a writing purpose. If such a book contains some mathematical charts, conversion tables or/and informative charts, these are some extra things that he gets. He doesn't pay an additional amount for these charts or conversion tables. They are additional benefits that the customer receives. Hence, it is a value addition from the point of view of the customer. Likewise, most producers give bonus packs to customers.

As well as value added to the product, it can be added to a service also. In addition to the direct service provided to the customer, the quality of the service can be enhanced by adding some features to the service.

For example, when a customer comes to the bank counter to withdraw money, the direct service is providing that service quickly. In addition, the counter person can greet the customer or he can ask about any other services which the customer requires. Seating arrangements can be provided. Reading materials can be made available or kept in the waiting area. Water dispensers can be installed in the waiting area. There are so many ways to satisfy the customer in addition to providing the direct service. Those are the main strategies to retain the customers within the organization. If an organization can retain customers successfully, it is one of the best ways of reaching higher productivity levels. Retaining existing customers is worth more than finding new customers. Gradually an organization can find new customers while retaining existing customers. The reputation of such organization spreads rapidly and it leads to the attraction of more new customers. Surveying customer satisfaction and asking them to pinpoint problem areas with services (or products) is a great way to make customers feel special, and valued. This helps with retention. It also provides excellent feedback to the organization and helps direct their energy to changes and improvements which add value.

We have discussed how to improve productivity in an organization. These concepts can be applied to an individual also. If any person tries to apply these concepts to his personal life, his life will also become more productive. That can be called personal productivity improvement. Personal productivity improvement can be done in two different ways, i.e., physically and mentally. If someone can maintain his physical appearance and health well, he will be productive physically. If someone can improve his mental quality, he will be able to be productive mentally. Then he will be able to manage his input output ratio productively and he will be able to succeed always. Therefore he should improve his physical and mental quality. Such people get a good reputation easily and such people are rich with good ideas and qualities. Such people may be said to have more value than average people.

For example, a person can get more knowledge with less effort. He is more productive than a person who gets more knowledge with more effort. He also can improve his skills in the same manner.

However, a person will not be successful by only having knowledge and skills. He has to improve attitudes also. If someone can improve more positive attitudes, he reaches to a higher productivity and quality level.

A doctor with medical knowledge and skills is not a complete person. He should have more positive attitudes to complete his skill set. A doctor with knowledge, skills and excellent attitudes will be treated as a quality person. Then he gets a good reputation automatically and finally he will be different from average people. This concept is applicable to any person.

So we can understand that the "productivity" word is universal. It can be applied everywhere, to every person, and every organization. However, the concept of input and output management, quality improvement, market promotion and value addition are the key points to improving productivity everywhere.

# CHAPTER 2

## Efficiency and Effectiveness

When the productivity concept is discussed in detail, there are two important words which cannot be neglected. They are efficiency and effectiveness. However, on some occasions these two words are interpreted incorrectly. Therefore, it is very important to understand the exact meanings of these two words.

## Efficiency

Efficiency means performing any task quickly. By increasing the speed of performing any task to maximum speed, efficiency can be increased. However, efficiency can be applied to any activity whether the activity is right or wrong, good or bad. For example, a gunman can handle the weapon quickly and shoot quickly. So his action is very fast. Therefore, someone could say that he is so efficient in shooting because he did the shooting very quickly. Nevertheless, no one can accept that it is a good task.

If a typist finishes his typing job quickly, he is considered to be efficient. However, the document may contain many typing errors. Although the typist is very concerned about his speed (efficiency), he is not concerned about the accuracy of the job.

A driver drives the vehicle to the expected destination within a shorter period of time. So he is efficient. However, he reaches the destination by violating road regulations, having some accidents. Although the driver drives efficiently he doesn't follow rules because his prime intention is to finish the job as quickly as possible. He is not concerned about the correct way of performing the task. Likewise a student can solve some mathematical problems within a given time. If the student can solve them within a shorter time period and accurately, he is also efficient.

Hence, it is understood that if someone can increase the speed of an activity, although it is right or wrong, efficiency of that activity is high. However, it is hard to say that activity is productive. Therefore, it is not correct to say that an activity or a person is productive although that activity or the person is efficient only.

## Effectiveness

Effectiveness means performing any activity accurately. If the accuracy of any activity is increased, effectiveness will also be increased. When accuracy is maintained properly, the possibility of doing wrong or bad activities is minimal.

If a typist types the document clearly and precisely without any typing mistakes and maintains typing standards, the accuracy of that document is high. So that task is effective. The typist is concerned about the accuracy of that task. However, he may not be concerned about the time taken to finish typing because he is concerned only about the effectiveness.

A driver drives the vehicle to the destination following all road regulations, very carefully and without any accidents. So the accuracy of his driving is high. However, he may take more time than expected to reach the end point. As he follows all correct procedures, he is accurate. It means he is effective.

Taking all the above mentioned examples into consideration, we can come to some conclusions. First, it is understood that maintaining effectiveness or efficiency alone is not productivity. In order to be productive, effectiveness and efficiency should be maintained simultaneously. For example if the driver can reach the destination as soon as possible following the road regulations, he can maintain effectiveness as well as efficiency. Then his driving can be considered as productive. Likewise, if the typist can type the document quickly and precisely without any errors, his typing will be productive.

Therefore, in order for an activity to be productive, first the right activity must be selected and then the right method should be followed. It means doing the right thing in the right manner. If the wrong activity is selected and performed in a wrong manner or the wrong activity is selected and performed in a right manner or the right activity is selected and performed in a wrong manner, each occasion will be unproductive. Hence, spending resources and investing money on such activities are not productive. In order to achieve expected goals productively, right activities should be identified and they must be implemented in the right manner.

# CHAPTER 3

## Productivity Comparison of some Countries

In order to measure the productivity levels in a country, different indicators are used. However, most countries frequently use per capita gross domestic product (GDP) to measure productivity because it is easier to understand by everyone. The GDP is the value of all goods and services produced by the total population of a country. By dividing the value of the gross domestic product by the population of the country, the per capita gross domestic product can be determined. In order to compare this value with the values of other countries, it is normally calculated in US dollars. But it can be calculated in the currency of any specific country.

The values of per capita gross domestic product of several countries have been illustrated in the following table in order to give you an idea. Try to analyze the changes that happened during the past 50 years. (The sources of these values are the World Bank, the productivity centres of each country and the Asian Productivity Organization.)

| Year / Country | 1960 | 1970 | 1980 | 1990 | 1995 | 2000 |
|---|---|---|---|---|---|---|
| Bangladesh | 85 | 135 | 225 | 286 | 323 | 364 |
| Canada | 2295 | 4047 | 10935 | 20968 | 20117 | 23560 |
| China | 92 | 112 | 193 | 279 | 604 | 949 |
| India | 82 | 110 | 263 | 363 | 369 | 437 |
| Japan | 479 | 1974 | 9171 | 24754 | 41968 | 36789 |
| Malaysia | 299 | 392 | 1803 | 2418 | 4287 | 4006 |
| Pakistan | 81 | 169 | 294 | 323 | 476 | 512 |
| Singapore | 394 | 925 | 4913 | 11845 | 22922 | 23815 |
| South Korea | 156 | 279 | 1674 | 6153 | 11468 | 11347 |
| Sri Lanka | 142 | 183 | 267 | 463 | 715 | 871 |
| Switzerland | 1787 | 3699 | 17383 | 35472 | 44873 | 34787 |
| Thailand | 101 | 192 | 681 | 1495 | 2817 | 1942 |
| UK | 1380 | 2242 | 9633 | 17688 | 19944 | 25083 |
| USA | 2881 | 4998 | 12180 | 23038 | 27559 | 35082 |
| World | 447 | 782 | 2473 | 4138 | 5197 | 5271 |

| Year / Country | 2005 | 2006 | 2007 | 2008 | 2009 | 2010 |
|---|---|---|---|---|---|---|
| Bangladesh | 429 | 435 | 475 | 547 | 608 | 675 |
| Canada | 35089 | 39250 | 43246 | 45100 | 39656 | 46212 |
| China | 1731 | 2069 | 2651 | 3414 | 3749 | 4429 |
| India | 738 | 822 | 1058 | 1021 | 1140 | 1410 |
| Japan | 35627 | 34148 | 34264 | 38212 | 39456 | 42831 |
| Malaysia | 5286 | 5890 | 6905 | 8099 | 6902 | 8373 |
| Pakistan | 691 | 789 | 871 | 979 | 949 | 1019 |
| Singapore | 28953 | 31519 | 36655 | 36738 | 37790 | 41120 |
| South Korea | 17551 | 19707 | 21653 | 19162 | 17110 | 20757 |
| Sri Lanka | 1230 | 1409 | 1596 | 1989 | 2035 | 2375 |
| Switzerland | 50083 | 52276 | 57490 | 65800 | 63568 | 67457 |
| Thailand | 2644 | 3078 | 3643 | 3993 | 3835 | 4608 |
| UK | 42569 | 40342 | 46123 | 42935 | 35129 | 36343 |
| USA | 37867 | 44695 | 46459 | 47015 | 45793 | 47153 |
| World | 7021 | 7522 | 8386 | 9097 | 8520 | 9175 |

TABLE 1

By analysing the per capita GDP values shown in table 1, it is clear that different countries have acquired different values every year. Meanwhile some countries have higher values and some other countries have comparatively low values. In addition, the rate of increase of this value is also different from country to country. If we compare the per capita GDP values of 1960 and 2010 of some countries, South Korea has multiplied it by 133 times, Malaysia 28 times, Singapore 104 times, Thailand 45 times, India 17 times and Sri Lanka 17 times. When our attention is focused to some western countries, even though the rate of increase is somewhat low, their per capita GDP values are very high even in the 1960s. The reason behind this is that such countries have gained higher per capita GDP levels even in 1960 and they were considered as developed countries.

By analysing the following graphs for per capita GDP pattern of each county, it is easy to understand how it fluctuated from 1960 to 2010.

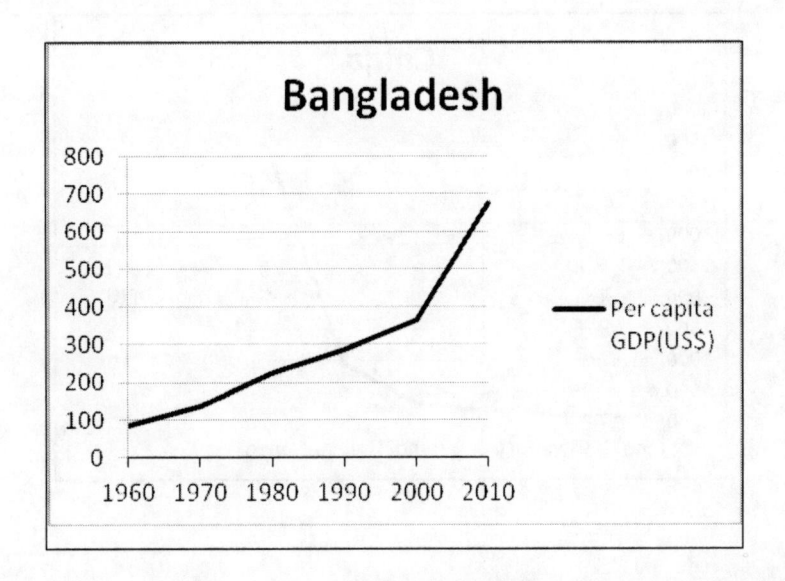

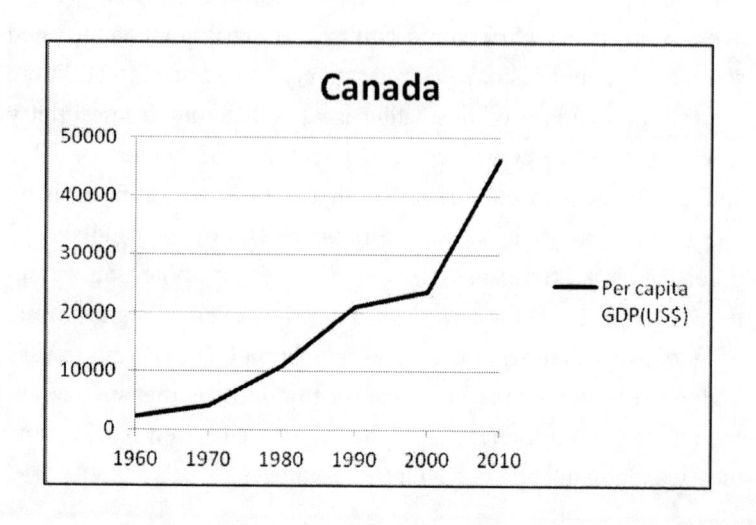

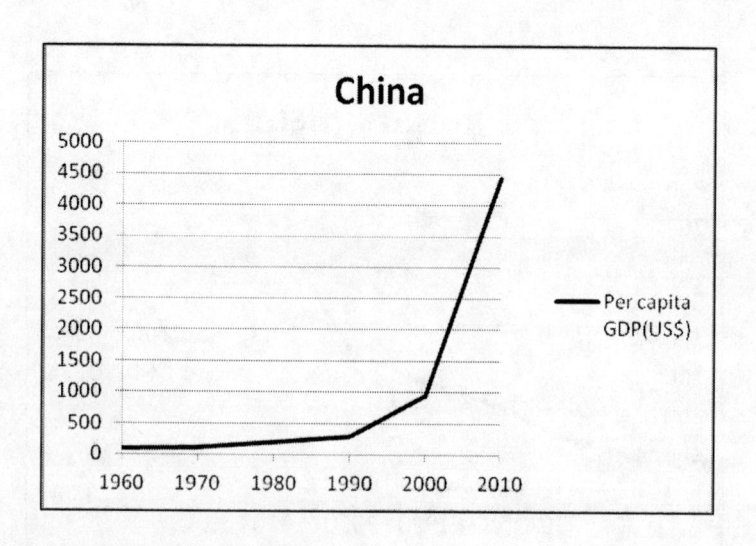

**Canada**

*Per capita GDP (US$) from 1960 to 2010*

**China**

*Per capita GDP (US$) from 1960 to 2010*

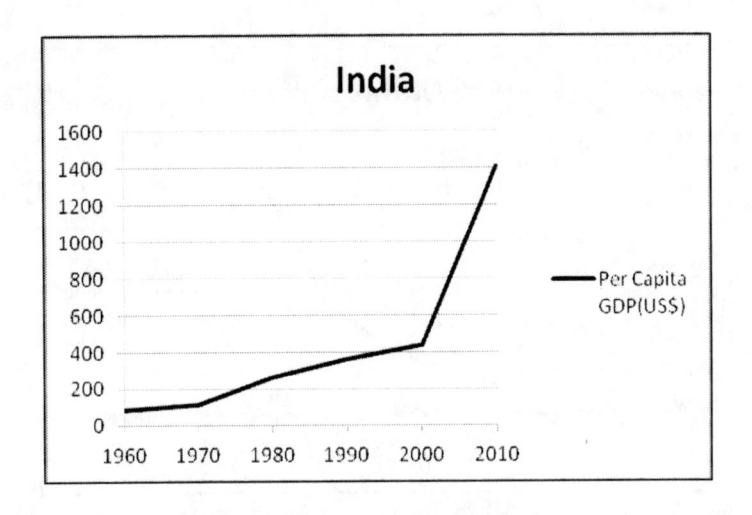

## India

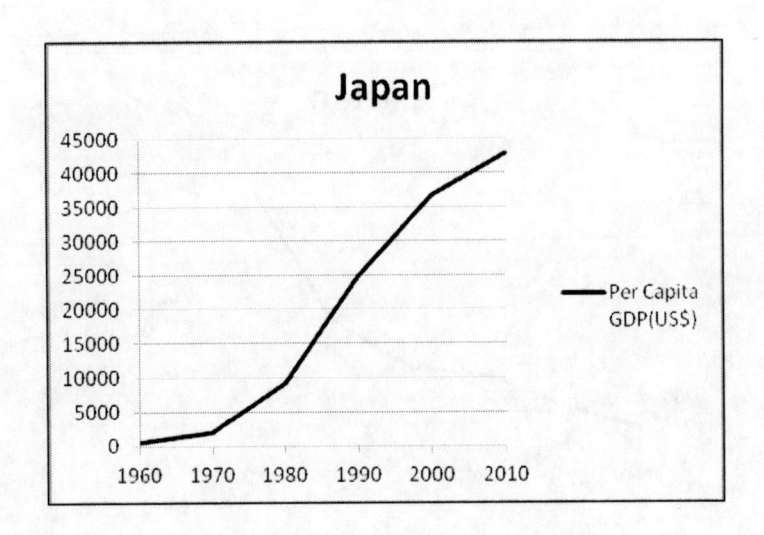

Per Capita GDP(US$)

## Japan

Per Capita GDP(US$)

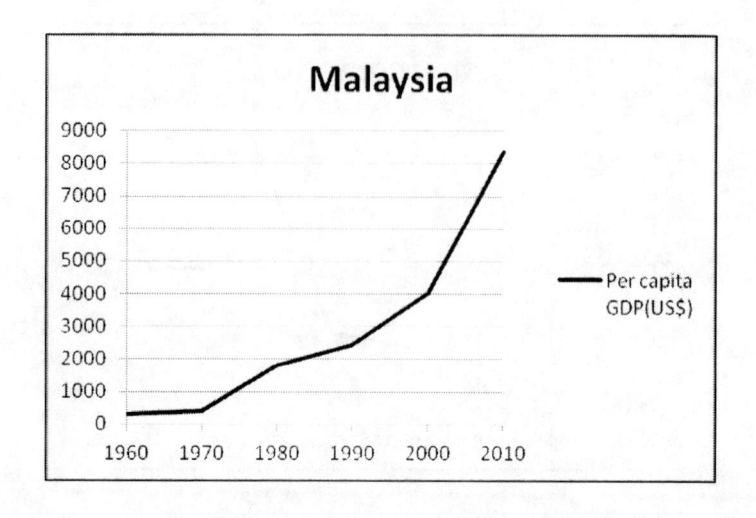

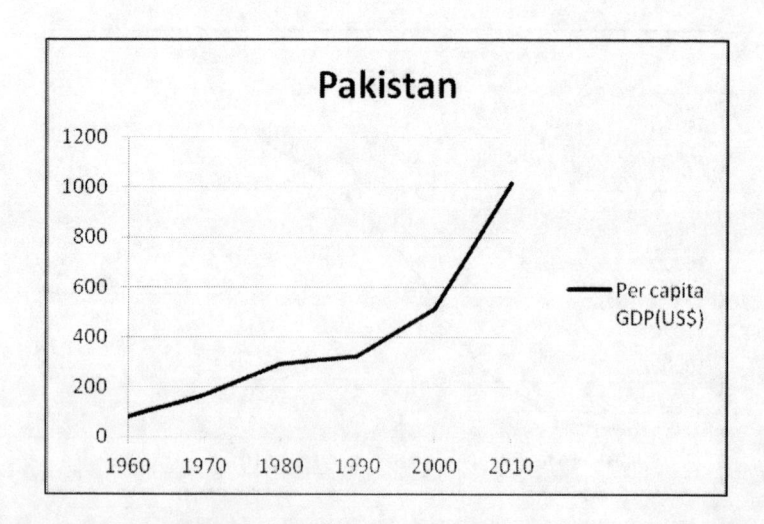

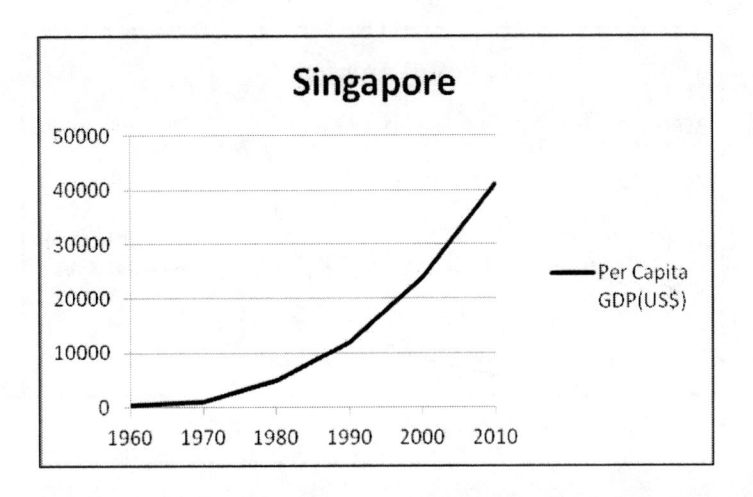

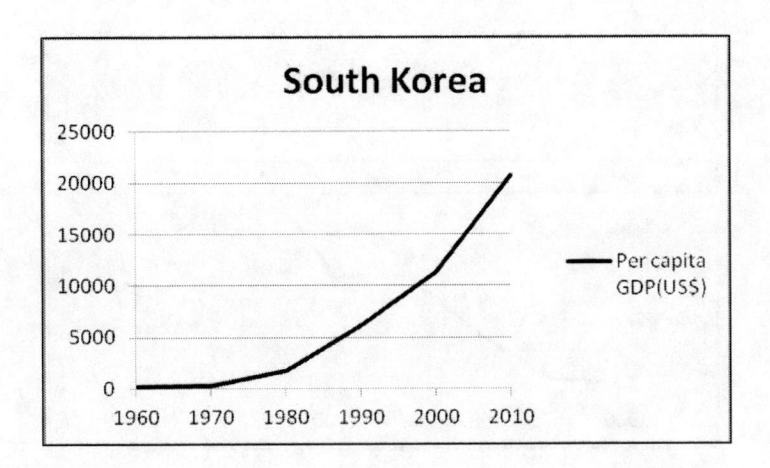

## Singapore

*Per Capita GDP(US$) chart showing growth from near 0 in 1960 to approximately 41000 in 2010*

## South Korea

*Per capita GDP(US$) chart showing growth from near 0 in 1960 to approximately 21000 in 2010*

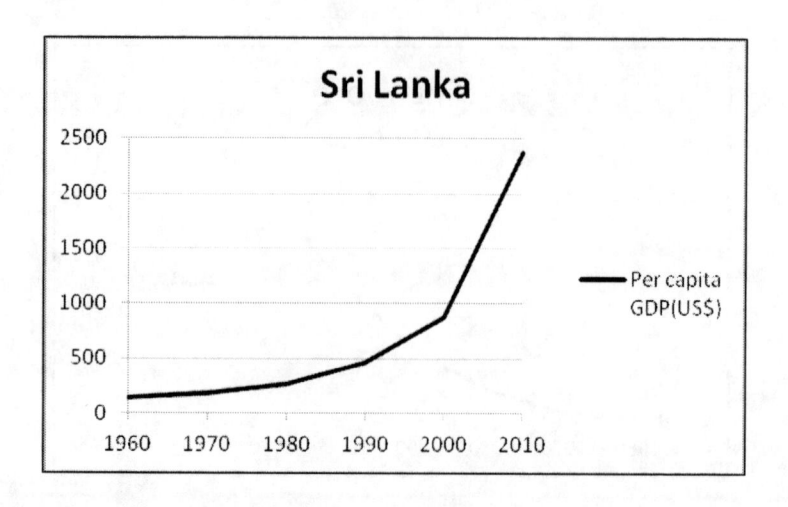

**Sri Lanka**

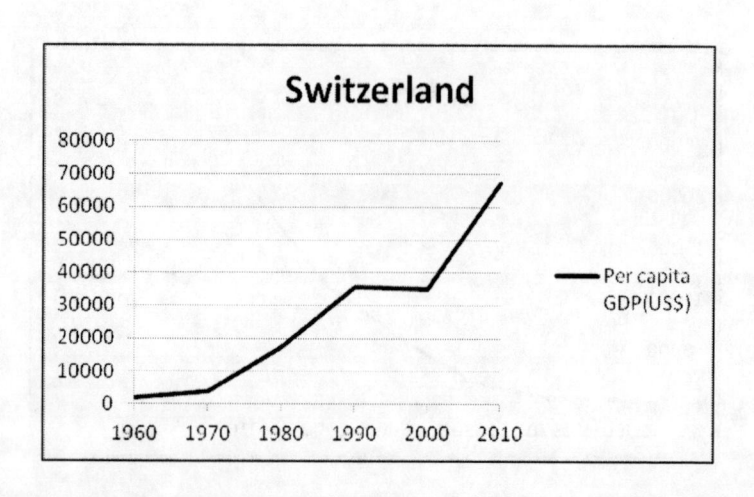

Per capita GDP(US$)

**Switzerland**

Per capita GDP(US$)

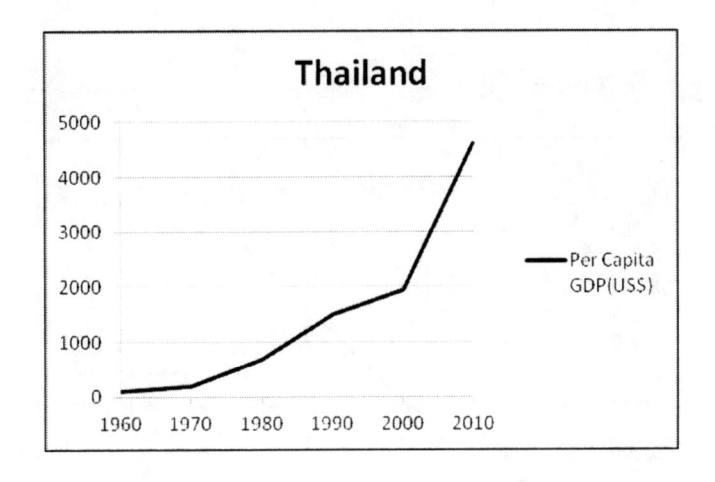

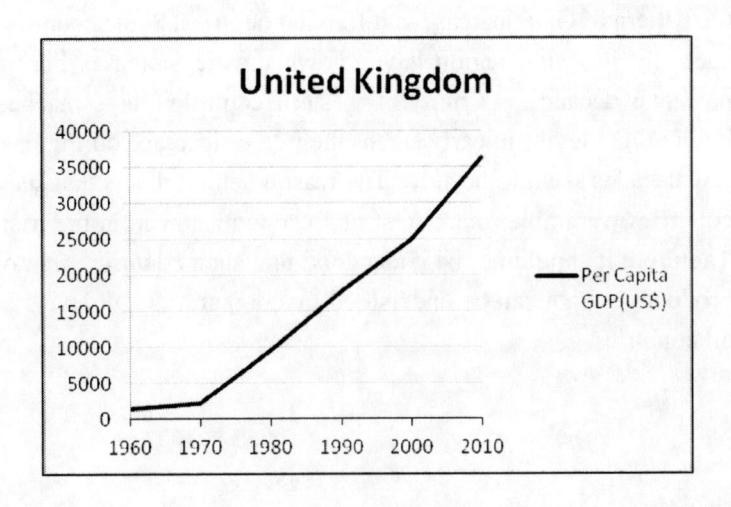

**United States**

*Per Capita GDP(US$)*

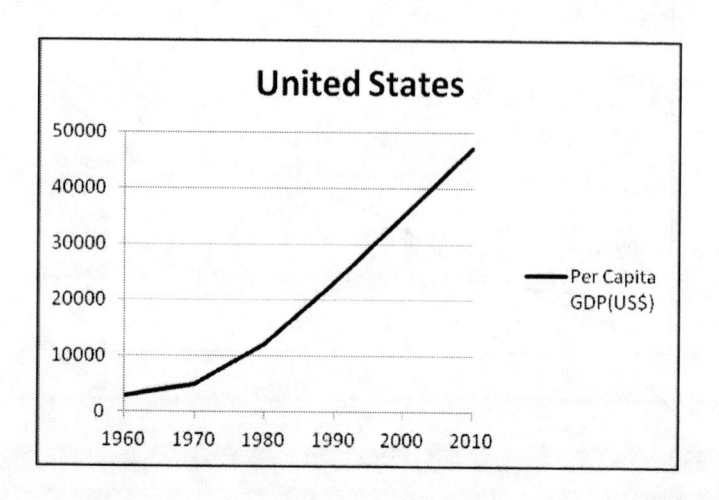

By analyzing all these graphs, it is easy to get a clear idea of the pattern of GDP increase in different countries. Some countries specially in Asian region have shown drastic increases during past two decades. As most of western countries have reached higher GDP levels in early stages the rate of increase during past few decades seem to be slow. The reason behind this is that such countries were able to create strong economies even in the past. Therefore it should not be understood that such countries are not productive. That can be understood by comparing GDP levels in all countries.

The following graph includes the per capita GDP patterns in all the countries considered for our study.

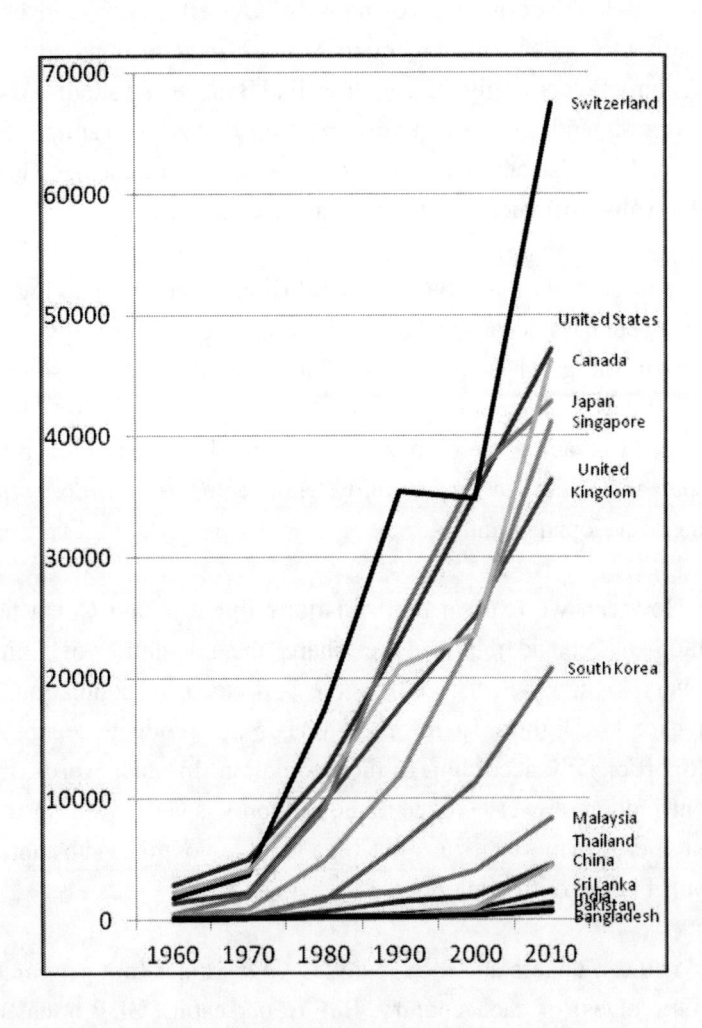

[Graph: Per capita GDP from 1960 to 2010 for multiple countries — Switzerland, United States, Canada, Japan, Singapore, United Kingdom, South Korea, Malaysia, Thailand, China, Sri Lanka, India, Pakistan, Bangladesh. Y-axis ranges from 0 to 70000.]

According to the graph, Switzerland has the highest per capita GDP value (year 2010) meanwhile Bangladesh has the lowest among the countries considered for the study.(In 2010, Luxemburg recorded the highest per capita GDP value among all the countries in the world.) This tells us that the contribution of each citizen to the economy in Switzerland is much higher that than in Bangladesh. It gives an idea how effectively and efficiently the citizens of such countries work and contribute to their economy. Accordingly the countries like Bangladesh should work more efficiently and effectively to reach higher per capita GDP levels. Likewise any person can study and compare the per capita GDP values of other countries to have a clear idea.

It is obvious that you have confusion about the ranking of these countries because China and India have acquired low positions in the graph even though China and India are considered as fast developing countries in the Asian region. Specially, China has been invading the global market which has been grabbed by Japan and South Korea. Currently China competes far more with other developed countries.

How can we explain this situation? Even though China has grabbed a considerable market share, the population of China is very high. When the GDP value is divided by population, it gives a low figure. Therefore, China is not productive enough proportionately according to the population. In other words, the contribution of every citizen to the economy is very low. It means that there are more citizens in China who do not make substantial contribution to its economy.

You can understand it by studying GDP values (not per capita GDP values) of each country. Before per capita GDP is calculated, GDP (Gross Domestic Product) value should be calculated. GDP is the gross value of all goods and services produced in a country during the year.

Let's analyse the GDP values of these countries for 2010 using the following table.

| Country | GDP in USD | Population | Per capita GDP |
|---|---|---|---|
| USA | 14,586,736,313,339.00 | 309,349,000 | 47,153.01 |
| China | 5,926,612,009,749.60 | 1,338,300,000 | 4,428.46 |
| Japan | 5,458,836,663,870.90 | 127,451,000 | 42,830.87 |
| UK | 2,261,713,093,830.20 | 62,232,000 | 36,343.25 |
| India | 1,727,111,096,363.30 | 1,224,615,000 | 1,410.33 |
| Canada | 1,577,040,082,217.80 | 34,126,000 | 46,212.27 |
| Korea | 1,014,483,158,313.60 | 48,875,000 | 20,756.69 |
| Switzerland | 527,919,933,356.40 | 7,826,000 | 67,457.19 |
| Thailand | 318,522,264,428.70 | 69,122,000 | 4,608.12 |
| Malaysia | 237,796,914,597.20 | 28,401,000 | 8,372.84 |
| Singapore | 208,765,019,307.70 | 5,077,000 | 41,119.76 |
| Pakistan | 176,869,569,654.00 | 173,593,000 | 1,018.88 |
| Bangladesh | 100,357,022,443.80 | 148,692,000 | 674.93 |
| Sri Lanka | 49,551,751,282.50 | 20,860,000 | 2,375.44 |

TABLE 2

According to the above table, China is the 2nd highest country (among the countries considered for this study) in GDP values whereas it records the 10th place according to the per capita GDP values in our study. Now it is understood that China has substantially higher GDP value but it computes to a lower value when it is divided by the population in order to calculate per capita GDP value. This means that the fraction of the population which contributes to the economy productively is lower than that of a country which has a higher per capita GDP value (year 2010) like Switzerland.

Switzerland has a value of per capita GDP of USD 67,457 which gives an idea that each citizen's contribution to the economy is much higher than that of developing countries. The fraction of population which contributes to the economy in Switzerland is much higher than that of other developing counties.

What would be the situation if each citizen in all countries contributed to the economy like citizens in the USA, Luxemburg and Switzerland? Their GDP values would be much higher. In order to have an idea, we can multiply the population of each country by the per capita GDP of Switzerland and calculate a hypothetical GDP value and compare how such countries could have reached maximum economic growth. Table 3 shows the hypothetical values of such GDPs.

| Country | GDP in USD | Population | Hypothetical GDP- $ M (Population*67457) |
|---|---|---|---|
| China | 5,926,612,009,749.60 | 1,338,300,000 | 90,277,703.10 |
| India | 1,727,111,096,363.30 | 1,224,615,000 | 82,608,854.06 |
| United States | 14,586,736,313,339.00 | 309,349,000 | 20,867,755.49 |
| Pakistan | 176,869,569,654.00 | 173,593,000 | 11,710,063.00 |
| Bangladesh | 100,357,022,443.80 | 148,692,000 | 10,030,316.24 |
| Japan | 5,458,836,663,870.90 | 127,451,000 | 8,597,462.11 |
| Thailand | 318,522,264,428.70 | 69,122,000 | 4,662,762.75 |
| United Kingdom | 2,261,713,093,830.20 | 62,232,000 | 4,197,984.02 |
| Korea | 1,014,483,158,313.60 | 48,875,000 | 3,296,960.88 |
| Canada | 1,577,040,082,217.80 | 34,126,000 | 2,302,037.58 |
| Malaysia | 237,796,914,597.20 | 28,401,000 | 1,915,846.26 |
| Sri Lanka | 49,551,751,282.50 | 20,860,000 | 1,407,153.02 |
| Switzerland | 527,919,933,356.40 | 7,826,000 | 527,918.48 |
| Singapore | 208,765,019,307.70 | 5,077,000 | 342,479.19 |

TABLE 3

If countries like Luxemburg, Switzerland, Japan and the USA can, why can't other countries? The above table shows that China's hypothetical GDP value would be the highest because

China has the highest population. If every citizen in China contributes to the economy like Switzerland, China's economic growth would be the No. 1 among all the countries.

Why can't the people in countries which have low per capita GDP contribute to their economies like developed countries? If all humans have more or less equal capacity, why is there such a difference in their effectiveness and efficiency? In order to have a clear answer for these questions, it should be analysed in the context of productivity development. In order to reach higher per capita GDP levels, resources should be managed effectively and efficiently (productively).

That means productivity improvement. Low productivity or GDP means lack of proper management of resources. Any country would have been among the countries in the top level, if every citizen had acted wisely by using productivity concepts properly.

Suppose a country which has a population of 20M and imagine that 10 million belong to the active work force. If 10 million people plant 10 million chili plants every year, the value of production is $ 2.00 x 10 million, i.e., 20 million US dollars. Planting a chili plant is very easy. Any citizen can do much more than planting a chili plant, such as working more in the factory, producing more units, working more productive hours, etc. That is how developed countries achieved higher productivity levels and developed such countries.

Another way of contributing to the GDP is sharing your knowledge and creating more skilled individuals because, by doing so, there may be more skilled people to contribute to the economy of the country. It is an indirect contribution to the GDP growth.

A person, who loves his country and performs his activities, whether they are personal or job-related, will be a good contributor to the GDP. Hence, it is a great responsibility of every citizen to perform any activity for the betterment of himself as well as others. If you don't take any activity of which you are capable, it can be considered as a crime to the common public and to the nation. If you do it at least at your capacity, it will be some sort of contribution. The time spent, even a single minute, on harmful, unethical and unproductive activities can be used to perform activities which are not harmful or unproductive. It is one way of contributing to the GDP.

By increasing the GDP, a country will have a strong economy. It means more money for development. Then the burden imposed on citizens would be minimal. If not, any government is compelled to impose burdens such as tariffs and taxes in order to maintain the administrative system, infrastructure, health, education systems, etc. Otherwise it is very difficult to develop a country.

What is the role of citizens in the process of improving per capita GDP in a country? Every citizen can contribute to increase the GDP in his country easily. For example, suppose you plant a single chili plant in your home garden on the 1st day of January. If it is maintained well, you can at least get a harvest of around 500 grams from that plant. If it is costed out, the value would be $ 2.00. That means you have contributed to the economy by creating $ 2.00. That is a contribution to the GDP. Likewise, if everybody contributes in the same manner, try to calculate the amount contributed to the GDP value every year.

A country lacking money for development activities will have to maintain its activities within a limited framework, so the lifestyle development in such a country will also be limited. Then the country will not be able to compete in parallel with other countries in a globalized economy. It closes doors to new technology, education and creative innovations.

On the other hand, there are many activities that damage the economy and GDP. For example, destroying public property intentionally or unintentionally damages the country's economy. It can be considered as a negative contribution to the economy and every citizen should take this into serious consideration because the government will have to divert its funds, which could be utilized for development activities, to renovate damaged property. Hence the responsibility of any citizen is to contribute to the economy at their capacity and refrain from performing unproductive activities including damaging public property, performing unethical activities, etc.

For our analysis, per capita GDP values of such countries were used. However, per capita GDP value is not the only value which is considered to determine the economic development of a country. You can realize this by focusing your attention on China. We observed that the per capita GDP of China is comparatively lesser even though China plays a vital role currently in the global economy. In addition, countries which have economies highly dependent on minerals such as oil may not show the real GDP value because the income generated from such minerals is also added to the total GDP value. So the figure may be distorted as it is not the contribution made by the citizens. In such situations, countries with citizens who work less can be ranked at a higher level than that they should be.

However, in order to get a general idea of economic development and how productive a country is, comparison of per capita GDP values is adequate. If someone needs to study in depth and to analyse them in the context of economics or in policy making levels, there are so many indicators.

The Global Competitiveness Report which is released annually is a good source to study and compare how countries have performed and played their role in the context of economic development. While the Global Competitiveness Report gives an overall ranking of the countries according to Global Competitive Index (GCI), it illustrates the performance of such countries in 12 different areas which are called as 12 pillars. They are Institutions, Infrastructure, Macroeconomic Environment, Health and Primary Education, Higher Education and Training, Goods Market Efficiency, Labour Market Efficiency, Financial Market Development, Technological Readiness, Market Size, Business Sophistication and Innovation.

As it is useful to have a general idea about these 12 pillars, each pillar in nutshell has been explained below.

**1. Institutions**

It is essential that any country should have a sound legal and administrative framework in order to run every sector smoothly. It is like a foundation of a building. If the foundation is weak, the possibility of collapsing is higher. Likewise, if the legal and administrative system is not strong, the possibility of collapsing the whole system including the economy is high and no institution can interact well in the process of economic development.

As far as the legal system is concerned, it should be totally independent from political or any other administrative influence. People should have a strong trust in the impartiality, equality and justice of the legal system. It should also be totally transparent. An independent legal system creates confidence among the public. Such an environment opens doors to anyone to invest in economic activities without hesitation and fear. It will be a strong motivating factor to attract investors.

In addition to the sound legal system, a country must have a people-friendly administrative framework. The prime feature of the administrative system is effectiveness and efficiency. The role played by the administrators is vital to facilitate and promote economic activities. Administrators should facilitate and provide their service to the investors or contributors in the economy in order to run their activities smoothly. Bureaucrats should be able to blast their so-called red tape, go beyond the written rules and regulations for the sake of the betterment of the society. They should always be aware of creating new sound policies with a long term vision. They should not stick to the old, outdated rules and regulations and they should have the sense to identify when policy changes are needed. Administrative systems should be productive in order to provide effective and efficient service to stakeholders. The service delivery time should be minimal and lengthy unnecessary procedures should be eliminated. Periodical improvements to the systems and work procedures should be introduced.

In addition, the possibilities for corruption should be eradicated. Corrupted systems should be re-engineered and new systems should be established. Corrupted officers should be removed and punished. Proper monitoring systems should be established. A productive and development-oriented administrative system as well as a development-oriented accounting system should be maintained. Rather than a traditional audit system, a productivity and development based audit system is a must.

Furthermore, sound financial planning and management is essential. The possibilities for gaining economic benefits should be identified periodically and financing on unsound, unproductive or less important activities should be stopped. Therefore, a well disciplined financial management system is a must to gain the expected benefits.

Taking all these factors into consideration, they can be summarised as good governance. The ultimate outcome of it should be a people-friendly, productive legal and administrative system.

## 2. Infrastructure

It is very clear that well-planned quality infrastructure facilities such as road network, railway system, telecommunication system, airports and ports, are essential prerequisite for economic development. A sound road network links urban and rural area easily and it tends to minimize the development gap between urban and rural levels. Investors can transport their products anywhere they want easily and quickly if the road network is well developed. In addition a sound public transport system eases employees to report to duty on time and it leads to eliminate wasting time during transit.

Proper ports and airport system open avenues to strengthen existing links and create new links with other countries. It encourages international business community to invest in such countries. If these facilities are not adequate, no one likes to invest money or to spend their time. The business community always tend to invest in countries which have sound infrastructure.

A well improved modern telecommunication system reduces the communication gap. Information can flow easily and smoothly to individuals. In addition the information flow will be very fast. Therefore, well developed infrastructure facilities act as impelling forces for investments and it leads to high economic growth.

## 3. Macroeconomic environment

In order to run an economic activity smoothly, the economic environment should be sound. It should cover all aspects of the economy. That's why the macroeconomic environment is very important to lead the country's economic growth towards a productive level. To create a sound economic environment, the fiscal policy of a country should be long term vision oriented, investor friendly and productivity oriented. Unstable, frequently vibrating, untrustworthy policies will harm the sound macroeconomic environment. If the macroeconomic environment is very strong and stable, obstacles for productivity improvement of a country would be minimal. It should be emphasized that the economic environment is very sensitive. Even one simple adverse activity may cause unforeseen tremendous effects on the economic environment and its effects and repercussions flow from the macro level to micro level also. The best example is the share market fluctuation when adverse policy changes are done or during some periods which the political stability prevails.

As long as the macroeconomic environment is sound, every economic activity operates well. Investors as well as beneficiaries are happy. Employees are also happy because the threat to their job security becomes minimal and their benefits would be protected. The positive effects of this penetrate to every individual in the society. Such type of situation leads not only to a sound economic development but also to social and cultural stability.

The ultimate cumulative effect of this situation would be a blessing to government. In addition, it will bring down the budget deficit which brings happiness to the rulers as well as citizens. Therefore, the policy makers must make every effort to create sound, practical, stakeholder friendly economic policies and such policies should be reviewed periodically and necessary changes should be introduced in a timely fashion.

## 4. Health and primary education

It is unnecessary to say that a healthy workforce is the most important resource to a country. If people are not healthy, a country gets a weak workforce. The workforce is one of the significant inputs in the context of productivity improvement. Therefore, an unhealthy workforce minimizes the quality and quantity of the final output. The rate of absenteeism of workers goes up. Ultimately the country gets very low production with low quality, which cannot compete with the products of developed countries. As an unhealthy workforce reduces the effectiveness and efficiency, the total productivity level also goes down.

In order to have a healthy workforce people should follow appropriate health habits and consume healthy food. In order to align people for such a healthy pattern, health education as well as health facilities should be improved. Therefore, the fund allocation for health should be a vital part. In addition continual attention should be given to health education and potential measures should be taken to maintain the health of the health system. Every possible step should be implemented to keep the citizens physically and mentally fit. Under the health education, prevention including safety should be given the priority rather than cure as cure costs more than prevention.

Primary education is another area which any country should give priority. Every citizen should have at least primary education. It leads to increase the literacy rate also. The final outcome of this is a capable workforce. Primary education enhances basic skills of every individual. Without having basic skills at least, it is hard to run an economy. However, the quality of the education as well as the depth of the content is very important as it is the foundational pathway to higher education. Having primary education, an individual would be able to manage day to day tasks and get solve minor issues himself. In addition they are connected with the work force in the country in a fruitful manner. Hence, health and primary education is a strong pillar in economic development.

## 5. Higher education and training

Even though the primary education is essential as discussed in point 4, primary education alone cannot make a considerable contribution to run the country's economy. Therefore, higher education and training is vital, for which a government should allocate more funds. It is a long term investment because it increases the quality and quantity of the human capital. Not like in the past, any country cannot have isolated economies because economic development has been globally networked. In order to keep strong links with the networked global economy, higher education and training is a must. Irrespectively if it is public service or private sector, employing well educated personnel is a vital factor on policy making and implementation to have a sound economic, cultural and social framework.

Under this education and training component, not only knowledge and skills but also attitudes should be developed. Then, a country can have better human capital with higher emotional capital. Without a positive emotional capital, the human capital has much less value. Therefore, human capital and emotional capital should be twined together to get the incredible output. A country needs more intellectuals to run the economy competitively and productively.

In addition, skill development of the workforce is essential. In order to develop skills of the workforce, training is a must and on the job training is vital. As the technology is moving fast daily, new technology has to be introduced in order to compete in the global economic development network. Therefore, skill development should also be given prior attention by heads of each organization. The share allocated from the budget of any organization should be considerably adequate to upgrade skills of each worker. However, allocating money is not adequate. Heads of organizations (management) should implement continuous training need assessments and employees should be oriented to such trainings. In order to get the real value of training allocations, well trained trainers, modern training facilities, encouraging workers, monitoring the progress and incentive schemes are also essential.

### 6. Goods market efficiency

A product whether it is a good or a service should be able to fulfil the customer expectation. Customer delight is more important and it is somewhat far above from the customer satisfaction. In order to have sound market efficiency, products should be delivered to the customers in a good manner. In this process quality of the product (good or service) is very important. As well as the quality, cost and delivery also should be in a customer-friendly manner. Products should be available according to the demand also. An environment to move products easily within the global network is a prominent feature.

In order to have such a system, background facilitation such as policy making, efficient and effective infrastructure systems are also vital. If government's intervention and influence in the operational activities is higher, it adversely affects the smooth market. That's why government's facilitation is very important. The laws or regulations which create a negative impact on the market efficiency should be modified and only practically sound rules and regulations should be taken into practice by the government.

Even though the taxation is a must to run a government, heavy taxes which could be harmful to the market efficiency should not be brought into practice. When government's adverse intervention is higher, the attraction of investors (foreign and local) goes down. Lengthy administrative procedures, bureaucracy, red tape, corruption and negligence act as impeding forces to the market efficiency. If market efficiency is strong, the transaction rate also escalates and it will bring benefits to the investors as well as customers.

## 7. Labour market efficiency

An efficient labour market is another important factor which a country should have to reach higher level of economic growth. It means the workforce members should be assigned or allocated exactly to the right job. Then, their maximum contribution can be obtained. If somebody is not for fit for the position, the output decreases. In addition, such persons are not happy with their job. Therefore, the right person for the right job is essential. That's how labour market efficiency can be maintained at higher levels. Hence, "fit the man to the job" concept is more important than "fit the job to the man" concept. "Fit the job to the man" concept is not productive and it consumes more resources without much productive outcome.

The other important feature under this topic is labour market flexibility. It means that the employees should be shifted or transferred from one activity to another activity or one job to another job easily. In order to do that, the skill range of workers should be vast and hence, workers should have the capability of performing different activities or jobs. However, this kind of phenomenon creates some social problems especially in developing countries. It may affect the sustainability of the government and its political system. Therefore, it has been observed that governments in most developing countries are a little bit reluctant to introduce such drastic changes because it may cause some unrest among the worker community. However, labour market flexibility is a must to reach high economic growth levels. By educating and providing appropriate training, such kind of resistance and fear can be eliminated gradually. In addition, motivation of employees and creating high morale among them create an easy environment to make such changes.

## 8. Financial market development

Every economic activity is based on finance. Without investing money, it is impossible to start or maintain a business. Normally, the financial market is mostly handled by banks, security exchanges and other government regulated financial institutes. Such kinds of organizations should also be very efficient and effective. In addition, these bodies should be investor friendly. As explained in point 1, the financial market should also be fully transparent. All systems such as deposits, withdrawals, loan facilities and international trade facilitation should be free from lengthy procedures. Long queues, long waiting times should be eliminated. Every step should be productive.

In addition, the financial market should also be expanded to remote area in order to connect remote level investors with the global business network. So micro financing is also as important as macro level financing. Honesty, freedom from corruption, trustworthiness, cordial customer relations etc., are vital qualities of a sound, investor-friendly finance market. Formulation of policies to create sound financial market is the sole responsibility of the government.

## 9. Technological readiness

Today, no one can survive forgetting the technological development. From birth to death, everyone is living with the technology. In order to go for higher economic development, technological development is a must. It reduces the time, effort as well as the cost; meanwhile it gives customer friendly products with high quality. Therefore, any country which wishes to succeed in the global economy should introduce modern technological development to every sector /area. Speed of introduction of technological changes drastically escalated after the 1980s because more technological innovation came out as a result of the development of information technology (IT/ICT). Today, any process of producing goods and services is linked with IT. In order to compete in the global market, the introduction of ICT is essential. Hence, any country who wishes to reach higher productivity levels, should promote IT.

In order to succeed in this challenge, ICT should be taught everywhere. It should be started from school level. Government institutions should be re engineered with ICT. Significant attention should be paid and potential measures have to be taken by the policy formulating bodies to encourage dissemination of ICT.

## 10. Market size

Even though production increases, it should have a good market. So the size of the market of each country is important. Big countries like the USA, have a large market size. However, small, developing countries have substantially small market size. However, such small countries also have the opportunity to expand their market size. In order to do that, they should expand their market to the international level rather than depending on the domestic market alone. In order to survive in the global market, the products should be of high quality and with competitive prices. Therefore, technological changes should be introduced and measures should be taken to maintain high productivity levels.

## 11. Business sophistication

In order to capture a large market size, business sophistication is also a strong factor. New business methodologies, strategies, should be adopted. In addition, high quality organizations are vital. Quality products, product variation, brand reputation, improved marketing strategies, excellent after sale services and a speedy delivery network are some of the strategies which any country can adopt to have business sophistication.

## 12. Innovation

By strengthening the above mentioned pillars any country can gain productive results. However, innovation can make an incredible contribution to the economic development of a country. Hence, every organization should take appropriate action to encourage innovations. Innovation means some inventions or some developments to the current products and presenting to the customers in a new fashion. It may be totally new or some improvements to the existing products (goods and services). However, the innovations should be customer oriented.

In order to do innovations, day to day research is compulsory. Hence, every country should encourage research in every sector and go for innovations. Innovations can change customers' buying pattern and customers can be diverted to innovative products. It definitely creates new market opportunities and it leads to increase profit.

A country which needs to improve its productivity should strengthen the above mentioned 12 pillars. These pillars create an environment for a strong sustainable and stable framework for development of a country. Every pillar is equally important and they cannot be separated. Each is a component in one system. However, the Global Competitiveness Report should be studied to get in depth knowledge about these pillars. This book intends to give only a general idea in order to augment the content of this book. Discussing the Global Competitiveness Report is not the purpose of this book.

As we have a general idea on the GCI, we can compare per capita GDP data and GCI data of the countries which we considered for our study. It can be observed that the ranking according to the per capita GDP and GCI is not the same.

| Country | Per Capita GDP -2010 | Global Competitiveness Index -2010 | Global Competitiveness Index -2012 |
|---|---|---|---|
| Switzerland | 67,457 | 1 | 1 |
| USA | 47,153 | 4 | 5 |
| Canada | 46,212 | 10 | 12 |
| Japan | 42,831 | 6 | 9 |
| Singapore | 41,120 | 3 | 2 |
| United Kingdom | 36,343 | 12 | 10 |
| South Korea | 20,757 | 22 | 24 |
| Malaysia | 8,373 | 26 | 21 |
| Thailand | 4,608 | 38 | 39 |
| China | 4,429 | 27 | 26 |
| Sri Lanka | 2,375 | 62 | 52 |
| India | 1,410 | 51 | 56 |
| Pakistan | 1,019 | 123 | 118 |
| Bangladesh | 675 | 107 | 108 |

TABLE 4

However, everybody should understand that these 12 pillars alone cannot convert a country to a productive level. In order to do that, productivity concepts and tools should be taken into practice everywhere. The use of productivity concepts gives fewer benefits if the above mentioned pillars are not strong enough to maintain the stability of the whole system of the country. The strength of these pillars strengthens the pavement to successful implementation of productivity concepts. So these pillars and productivity concepts can be treated as the bark and the core/heartwood of a tree.

So what would be the reasons for such a development or productivity gap among these countries? Different countries may give different reasons. They can highlight war situation, droughts, floods, earthquakes, tsunamis, etc., as reasons. However, some countries which have high GDP per capita figures have also faced such situations more or less. Therefore, no country can give such causes as reasons for the drawback of their countries. This argument applies not only to a country but also any minor organization within the country.

So what are the real causes for low productivity or development? Such countries do not perform at their full capacity or they do not have much capacity due to various reasons. They do not follow productivity principles accordingly. They could have contributed to the economy more than they did if they followed productivity principles. The responsibility of this fault equally goes to every citizen in the country.

**Why couldn't they perform well?**

The main reason is the lack of using productivity principles. Although high productivity levels can be observed in some organizations, it is not adequate to change the whole system because the number of such organizations is very small. The productivity principles should be applied to the main sectors which make substantial contributions to the economy. Such type of effort can be observed only on a few occasions in less developed countries. As a result of this, the income level of the citizens has gone down when compared to other developed countries. The direct impact of this situation is a low standard of living with poor health conditions. Hence, savings and investments have become minimal. People are not socially reliable. The countries which achieve higher productivity levels entertain a high standard of living as well as sound social status for their citizens.

There is an urgent need to introduce productivity concepts to every sector in developing countries. Even in developed countries which productivity concepts have already been implemented in vast scale, the implementation of productivity concepts can be further strengthened and expanded to drive towards the excellence as the excellence has no limits or boundaries. More awareness programs, demonstrations and training can be used as modes of implementing these concepts country-wide. However, it has been observed that most people do not have a clear idea of productivity concepts. This creates a negative impact and acts as a barrier to successful implementation of productivity concepts in many organizations. Some people are reluctant to accept and implement productivity concepts because of the myths created due to faulty understanding of these concepts.

# CHAPTER 4

# Myths about Productivity

Several myths can be observed which were created by different parties:

## 4.1. Implementation of productivity concepts leads to trimming the workforce

Because of this myth, most employees are reluctant to implement productivity concepts in their organizations and do not allow even the management to do this. They are more concerned about job security than productivity improvement. Productivity concepts do not mean trimming employees but they stress the need of deployment of employees productively. Hence, training of employees to perform activities with less effort is one way of introducing productivity into organizations. Management should educate employees and try to eradicate the false fear of employees.

For example, a knife or an axe can be used to cut a huge tree. However, using an axe would be more productive. However, we should not use either the knife or the axe because a chain saw surpasses both the knife and the axe in effectiveness and efficiency. If the chain saw is used, the time taken to cut the same tree will be less. Thus, in order to perform the same task we can use different tools and it can be performed with a different amount of effort. Using the chain saw is the best way because it requires less time and effort.

In addition, a machine which prints 25,000 copies per hour is more productive than a machine which prints 5,000 copies per hour. Such types of illustrations using similar examples should be inculcated into the minds of employees in order to eradicate this myth about productivity.

### 4.2. Productivity is a way to exploit labour

Paying lower wages and demanding more work is exploitation of labour. By implementing productivity concepts in an organization, employees can perform their duties with less effort and they can do more work during the specified time period. By performing more work the production of the company goes up. Then it leads to higher income. A part of the extra income can be used to increase the salaries as well as the other benefits such as bonuses, welfare facilities, etc. of employees. Hence, additional income to the organization means additional benefits to employees.

## 4.3. Productivity concepts create excess work

If an activity can be performed in less time than the specified time for that task, there is a time saving. Most employees have a fear that they will have to perform additional tasks during that saved time. Definitely the time saved can be used for more duties but with payment to compensate for it. Then the income level of employees goes up and they will be happy. Under the productivity concept implementation, more work means more money for employees. The indirect result of this is increased production. An increased production of an organization contributes to the total production of the country. It means a hike in GDP.

In a country where people work less, the development is also lower. When development is lower, the treasury will be emptier. When the treasury is empty, there are minimal opportunities to invest in development activities. Then the status of public necessities such as education, health, highways, etc. becomes very poor. It means a less developed country. Therefore, it is clear that less work leads to an underdeveloped country.

If employees in a country reject work or perform less work stating that the salaries are low, the development goes down because production decreases. That reduces the money going to the treasury indirectly. With a poor treasury, how can the salaries of employees be increased? It is a very difficult task and beyond the principles of economics.

The ultimate result of such a situation is low GDP. After the Second World War, the Japanese work force performed their duties even with low salaries in order to develop their country. Then production went up and the total income of the country escalated a substantial amount. As a result the workers got higher salaries. Because of higher salaries, all workers were compelled to work more. Gradually Japan was able to achieve remarkably high productivity levels. In addition to Japan, the best examples for such type of achievement in the Asian region are Singapore, South Korea and Malaysia. You can get more in-depth knowledge by studying per capita GDP values and analysing competitiveness reports which are issued annually.

When less work is performed, there is a vicious circle which everyone should study well.

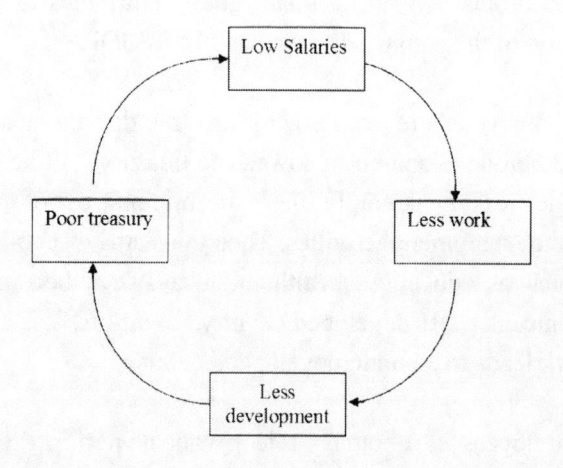

```
              Low Salaries
           ↗              ↘
  Poor treasury          Less work
           ↖              ↙
              Less
              development
```

Unless this cycle is broken productively, GDP and individual wealth will never increase. If work done is reduced continuously because of low salaries, it leads to poor development and the ultimate result would be a consistently poor country.

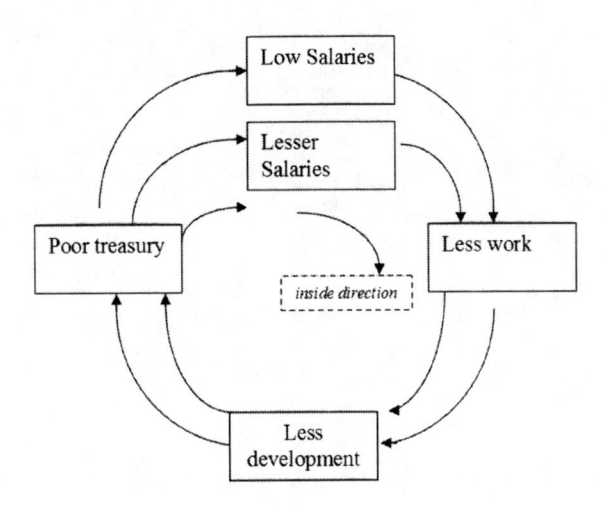

```
            ┌──────────────┐
            │ Low Salaries │
            └──────────────┘
            ┌──────────────┐
            │   Lesser     │
            │   Salaries   │
            └──────────────┘
┌──────────────┐            ┌──────────────┐
│ Poor treasury│            │  Less work   │
└──────────────┘            └──────────────┘
            ┌ inside direction ┐
            └ ─ ─ ─ ─ ─ ─ ─ ─ ┘
            ┌──────────────┐
            │    Less      │
            │ development  │
            └──────────────┘
```

*Breaking the vicious circle inside direction*

As illustrated in the above diagram, a low amount of work leads to low development. Low development dictates a poor treasury. Then salaries cannot be increased. If this continues again and again, the result will be a severe recession.

Developed countries always tried to break this vicious circle in an outside direction. After the Second World War, the Japanese increased the work volume in spite of low salaries. Because of the increase in work volume, the production volume went up and income escalated. So they owned a rich treasury and then the salaries were increased. Gradually the Japanese workers understood that the way to increase income is through increasing production. As a result of the high volume of work, the GDP went up gradually. This methodology has been adopted by developed countries and they have gained remarkable productivity levels.

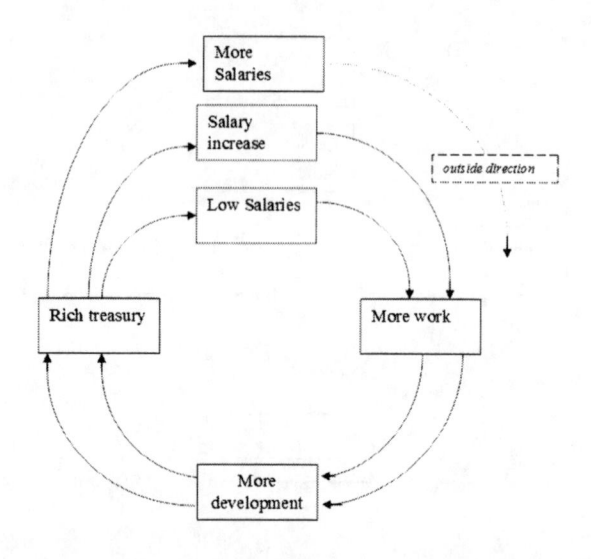

*Breaking the vicious circle in an outside direction*

If there is no development in a country, any government or any organization cannot increase salaries. Even if the salaries can be increased artificially, it will create more adverse effects to the economy. Inflation goes up. Hence, it is understood that the only way of having higher salaries and a higher standard of living is to improve production while maintaining higher productivity levels. It means an increase in Gross Domestic Product.

### 4.4. Productivity concepts create more hardships on the job.

There is another myth that productivity means working very hard. This is completely wrong. If someone works overly hard, that means he is not applying the productivity concepts into the work process. If you can perform any difficult job more easily by applying different methods, that is the application of productivity principles. Productivity is not working harder but working smarter. Increasing work volume by using easier methods means productivity improvement. But forcing employees into a difficult working environment does not lead to productivity improvement. Perhaps it may create frustration among employees and that will lead to poor production with poor quality.

For example, if a worker transports 50 cement bags by lifting them himself, he will have to make a great effort. If he uses a wheelbarrow to transport the same number of cement bags, he will be able to do it with less effort and within a shorter time period. Using a wheelbarrow is a more productive method than lifting. Hence, time can be saved and this time can be utilized for another productive task.

In addition, returning to the scenario of cutting a huge tree using a knife, an axe or a chain saw: Using the chain saw is the most productive method. Productivity improvement does not mean harder jobs; productivity is making the job easier by using different kinds of tools and techniques.

## 4.5. By implementing productivity concepts, workers lose their free time

Workers have another fear that they will lose their free time because of productivity improvement. They believe that they will have to work longer hours in order to increase productivity. Productivity concepts require you to plan your job very well. It introduces so many easy methods to perform a job. By using easy methods, time can be saved. Thus there is no reduction in the free time which employees enjoy. What is the point of having free time without performing your job well? First we have to perform the job well and then we can enjoy the free time as well-earned. The application of productivity concepts paves the way to finish your job in a timely fashion with less effort.

## 4.6. The application of productivity concepts creates strict discipline within the organization.

It is a must that there should be a proper management system in an organization and all members of the organization should behave according to the policies specified. Punctuality, decent behaviour, having reasonable break times, and contributing to a harmonious environment, are some of them.

If everyone is at his own workstation at starting time, this is a good indication of a productive organization. If someone comes late to the job, it affects everybody's job and the whole work process. Hence, total productivity output also gets affected.

According to the productivity principles, maintaining such a system cannot be stated as strict discipline. In order to maintain the organization, there should be clear and reasonable work ethics and standards. Having such a system, any organization can steer towards success. If workers are satisfied in the organization, they are very happy and they will be very proud to be members of that organization. If they are proud of their organization, the possibility of incidents where discipline fails is very low. Thus management does not face many such problems.

On some occasions, some employees have a habit to come late and cover the late time at the end of the day. Although it is acceptable, that may damage the overall performance of the organization. If such an employee performs his duties at the individualistic level, the harm is less. If that employee is in a key position of a process, the harm is vital because, in the absence of that employee, the whole process gets affected. It leads to decreasing the production volume. However, the flexible hours concept is very popular in western countries. Flexible hours mean that workers can select the shift or working time convenient for them. Then they come to work at a specific time which they select and work, and "normal" office hours are different from employee to employee.

However, the flexible hours concept cannot be applied to an organization where there is a production line because in the production line, all key workers have to operate the machines or perform activities to implement the process smoothly. However, in other areas like the office, the flexible hours concept is possible. In addition, if someone has to perform duties on a quota basis, he also can use flexible hours. Whether it is a flexible hours or normal office hour system, management has to plan work in a productive manner.

In most organizations success depends on the team effort. Everybody should work together in order to get the maximum output. Especially in a production process, everybody should be on time.

In order to sustain the system without any disturbance, this kind of system is a must. If the top level management, including the CEO of the organization, follows the rules and regulations, others feel compelled to stick to them. If the CEO comes to the workplace early, others will do so. If he gets in late, others also try to come late for their duties. This is common for any organization including the public sector and private sector.

Furthermore, discipline, in the sense of productivity, is not the discipline imposed by the top level management. It is self-discipline. It means you should have some built-in standards which should not be imposed from outside. It is advisable for every employee to have self-discipline, which leads to a successful organization.

# CHAPTER 5

# Benefits of Productivity Improvement

Anyone can obtain the benefits of productivity improvement communally and individually if productivity improvement prevails everywhere including the workplace, home, etc. In order to maintain higher productivity levels, everyone has to consume resources productively. Then the wastage of resources and defects which lead to high costs and adverse results can be avoided. Productivity improvement increases both tangible and intangible benefits.

If you return to the example explained earlier on planting chili plants, we calculated the amount of money that can be contributed to the economy if everyone in the active workforce planted at least one chili plant per year. That was $ 20M. If you plant four chili plants per year, the estimated contribution to the production will be $ 80M. It is an increase of GDP by $ 80M. Compare this with the cost of some development projects in your country. Then you will be able to understand how such a small contribution makes a vital impact on the economy of a country.

Now you can understand that the GDP can be improved in many ways. The time spent in an ad hoc manner can be utilized to read a book, plant a seed, and by doing so, you can contribute to increase the GDP directly and indirectly. The ultimate result of all these contributions is increased national wealth.

As discussed earlier, one direct result of the increased national wealth is an increase of salary or income of the citizens. When productivity is improved, citizens can get a good income which is higher than their expenditures. The result of the higher income is an increased standard of living with some saving. Citizens can enjoy good food, clothes, shelter and many other facilities satisfactorily.

In most developed countries, most of the citizens can enjoy their lives affordably. Not only in western countries but also in Asian countries like Japan, Singapore, Malaysia and Korea, the populations achieved satisfactory levels and the citizens of these countries also enjoy many benefits of the productivity improvement. The main cause behind this is the dedication of citizens to the development of GDP. As far as some developing countries are concerned, it is hard to observe such a satisfactory situation currently like in Japan. A few people enjoy benefits, but the majority is not in a position to enjoy a good level of standard of living. If developing countries can improve their productivity level, not only in the workplace but also at the household level, everyone can enjoy more benefits.

Citizens with a good standard of living consume healthy foods and maintain good hygienic conditions. This definitely leads to a healthier nation. A healthier nation is the most important asset to a country because only healthy people can contribute more to the GDP improvement. If people are healthier, the government can reduce the money invested in the health sector and the excess amount of money can be diverted to develop the country. Building a healthy nation means the country has a strong workforce which can vitally contribute to the GDP.

It is very easy to understand the difference when the situation in countries like Somalia or Ethiopia is observed. The majority of citizens in these countries are not in a position to earn enough for their day-to-day basic requirements. They are also suffering from malnutrition which increases the probability of the spread of disease and early death. How can such a nation contribute to the economy of their country? How can they cultivate the fields or work in the factories? The people in such countries have to make a great effort to alleviate poverty in their countries. If any country is not concerned about productivity, such a country will also have to face hard economic recessions.

Taking all these factors into consideration, we can come to a conclusion that the end result of productivity improvement is a quality lifestyle with a peaceful society. A place where there is a good lifestyle is full of happiness. In a place where there is happiness, the unrest is minimal. The country in the Asian region which understood this situation first is Japan. The Japanese government took every measure to keep its citizens happy by managing productivity in all sectors. The Japanese government was concerned not only about the salaries and facilities of the people but also about the whole environment. All infrastructures were maintained properly and the environment was modified. Even today the Japanese are very concerned about the environment and most productivity practitioners advise to start applying productivity concepts to the environment. Even while you are walking on sidewalks, traveling in a train or traveling in a bus, everywhere you can enjoy an interesting environment. Roadsides have been maintained very well with flowering plants, trees, etc. The secret behind this is that a beautiful environment creates a sound mindset.

*Roadsides in some developing countries*

*Roadsides in some developing countries*

*Roadsides in developed countrie*

The photograph below illustrates how the railway station is maintained. Everything is in order, clean and equipped with modern facilities.

*Railway stations in less developed countries*

*Railway stations in developed countries*

*Automated ticketing machines*

*Automated entrance*

In developed countries, the road network has also been planned well. Sidewalks for pedestrians, safe crossings and adequate lanes for vehicles have been built properly with appropriate road signs. In addition, plants and trees have been grown to give a pleasant look as well as to reduce the pollution. As trees can absorb polluting particles in air it is a strong remedy to reduce pollutants in urban areas. Therefore, urban planners' responsibility is to take these facts into consideration when cities are designed.

*Well-planned roads*

*Well-planned roads*

When any country increases its economic activities, a modern road network gives a tremendous contribution. Such a system should be planned to minimize unnecessary congestion and waiting times because waiting during transport is not a value added activity. It increases the cost and such costs also added to the price of goods and services. If a product is costly, customers' attraction decreases. So multiple highways and crossovers can reduce such delays by a substantial amount. Even though such construction is very expensive, it is a wise investment on a long term basis.

*Highways*

Using space productively is also very important. Even if a county has more space, it should not use it unproductively. Specifically, deforestation for development projects should be carefully considered. Reserving forests as much as possible is the most productive measure because forests are the main source of water which is the prime need of the life. So moving to high rise building is a very productive way of saving space. One country which uses space wisely is Singapore. Even though Singapore does not have big forests, they plan growing trees as much as possible even with building complexes.

*High-rise buildings*

*Tree planting in community areas*

Developed, modernized systems without disturbances create a sound mind and it leads to high morale. The citizens in such an environment are likely to perform their day to day work efficiently and effectively because of fewer worries. Therefore, productive thinking and planning in every aspect is essential and important.

# CHAPTER 6

## Sectors of Productivity

When productivity is analyzed, it can be divided into four sectors.

### 6.1. Material productivity

Material is a very important input which should be handled wisely. Under the material productivity, the tangible amount of units that can be produced by a specific amount of materials is calculated. For example, the numbers of cups of tea that can be produced by one kilo of tea or the number of nails that can be produced using one kilo of iron are measured and then material productivity can be calculated.

However, it is very important to keep in mind that the standard and specific amount of inputs should be used. It is not allowed to reduce the amount of minimum inputs which have to be used and artificially increase the number of units.

Suppose 100 nails are produced by using 1 kilogram of iron and it means 10 grams of iron are needed to make one nail. If 10 grams of iron should be used to produce the nail, it is not allowed to reduced the weight of each nail and produce more units. The quality of nails should not be reduced. Keeping these factors in mind, the maximum output should be achieved by maximum input. The point stressed here is minimizing waste. Using the raw materials properly, maximum productivity levels can be maintained. It is material productivity.

## 6.2. Labour productivity

The number of labour hours or number of labourers used for a specific task can be treated as labour productivity. In order to increase the labour productivity, the units per labour hour can be increased or the number of labourers for a specific task can be reduced. Many steps can be taken to increase labour productivity. Paying incentives according to the piece rate system can be implemented. In addition, other motivation methods can be used to encourage workers in order to increase production. Carrying out process analysis and managing the number of workers is another way of improving productivity. Increasing pride of workmanship and creating high morale among employees are strong motivating factors for improving labour productivity.

## 6.3. Energy productivity

The energy crisis has been escalating unexpectedly and every country has faced a struggle for energy sources. However, day by day, energy sources are decreasing and prices of such resources are going up drastically. Hence, the energy factor creates a vital impact on productivity improvement. Therefore, energy saving and conservation in production processes is another way of maintaining productivity levels. As every process consumes energy, minimizing the number of units of energy and producing more units is the main point of energy productivity. The number of kilometres that can be traveled using one litre of gasoline (petrol) or the number of units that can be produced out of a specific amount of electricity units are some of examples for energy productivity. Using energy productively by reducing wastage leads to an increase of energy productivity. Therefore, every type of measure should be taken to adopt energy efficient methodologies.

## 6.4. Capital productivity

The financial value of any activity is considered under "capital productivity". It means the financial value of outputs is divided by the financial value of the inputs. Any organization or a person should take material productivity, labour productivity, and energy productivity into consideration. Finally, all these values are considered under capital productivity because ultimate success is measured in financial values. In order to reach capital productivity, every kind of cost should be taken into consideration. In addition to minimizing the input cost, reducing damages, reducing rejected items and wastes in every place should be decreased and other operational and administrative costs should also be minimized.

# CHAPTER 7

# Areas to be focused on in Productivity Improvement

Having knowledge of productivity concepts is not adequate enough to make an organization productive. Putting all these concepts into practice is a must and it is very challenging. There are many areas that have to be given more focus in order to transform an organization's productive level. Let's consider these areas one by one.

**7.1. Physical environment of the workplace.**

A sound work environment in the workplace is very important to maintain a higher productivity level of the workers. Appropriate lighting, adequate ventilation and minimal noise are some of the main points which should be looked into. Low intensity lighting reduces the speed of production because workers cannot see properly. In addition, such situations lead to accidents in the workplace and this has an adverse effect on productivity. The proper intensity of lighting should be maintained in order to keep workers productive and healthy.

For example, if there is improper lighting in a garment factory, operators cannot see the needles and then their fingers may be stitched accidentally. Such situations create a fall in production and increase the cost of medical expenses. Also, this lowers the morale of all other workers and their work may also go down in fear of another accident. So the organization is affected in several ways which lowers the productivity of the organization.

*Pleasant workplace*

*Well illuminated garment factory*

*Well illuminated bank*

Proper ventilation is another factor which controls production and productivity. If there is not a good ventilation system, the temperature of the work environment goes up. The percentage of carbon dioxide goes up. It creates poor conditions for workers such as sweating, dizziness, etc. Such situations also badly affect production because no one can pay full attention to the job due to the unpleasant conditions. In fact, illnesses in the staff can also emerge, causing higher absenteeism.

Noisiness also affects the levels of production because workers cannot concentrate their minds on the job. So, noisiness should also be reduced in a work environment. However, sound can be used as a motivator on some occasions. For example, light music, which creates a positive impact on workers, contributes to minimize fatigue and boredom. It also reduces mental stress. In some factories and other workplaces, it can be observed that light music is played to create an attractive environment for workers.

*Music system fixed in an office*

The end result of proper lighting, ventilation and music is a mentally motivated workforce. Such a workforce contributes to the achievement of goals of the organization better than a workforce where there is not such a pleasant environment.

## 7.2. Work setup

Proper work setup is another area to be developed in order to reach high productivity levels. Before work is started, every item which is needed should be set up in order. In addition, appropriate instruments should be in the work station. Outdated equipment, which causes slowdowns in productivity, should be replaced with modern, effective and efficient instruments.

For example, a computer is more productive than a typewriter. A whiteboard is more productive than a traditional blackboard. Overhead projectors and multimedia projectors are the most effective and efficient instruments currently in the classroom. Hence, setting up the workplace with appropriate equipment and locating them in appropriate places contributes to productivity improvement because such a setup reduces unnecessary time consumption as well as unnecessary operations which will be discussed later in more detail.

*Well planned work set up*

### 7.3. Work methods

Having a proper work setup as explained above is useless unless there are proper work methods. Workers should be aware of the most productive ways to perform any job and it is a responsibility of the management to introduce appropriate work methods and adequate and effective training in their use.

For example, using a chain saw rather than using a knife or an axe to cut a huge tree is a more productive work method. Management should replace axes or knives with chain saws and they should be introduced to the workers with effective training. In the past, banks used manual methods to write the addresses of account holders to send their monthly statements. Now the 'mail merge' system has been introduced and it is a speedy and productive work method.

When big projects are implemented, network analysis or critical path analysis is used as a good method of planning the implementation part of the project. By using this method the time taken for more activities can be reduced and multiple activities can be performed simultaneously. This type of approach reduces time, saves money and resources and minimizes unexpected waste. Therefore, the management of the organization should be alert to the new innovations to update the work methods and work setup in order to favourably compete with others.

## 7.4. Proper arrangement of workplace

Every item in the workplace should be arranged properly in order to use it easily. It is necessary to study the workplace and locate all items in appropriate places. This type of arrangement minimizes the handling time, movements, etc. By doing so, unnecessary equipment can be removed and unnecessary activities can be eliminated.

For example, a clerk has to travel a long distance if his filing cabinet is kept far away from his work station. If he has to travel frequently to take files from the cabinet, it is obvious that he is spending more time on traveling between his work station and filing cabinet than necessary, taking time away from performing his actual duties. By locating the filing cabinet near to the work station in a convenient place, the time can be utilized for any other productive task. Likewise, stationing all the staff members in appropriate places and locating equipment accordingly, productivity can be increased because it helps to reduce unnecessary movements and unnecessary activities. Another example is locating printers and photocopiers in offices. Printers and photocopiers cannot be allocated for each employee in the office. Such items have to be shared. So such items should be located in a place where each employee can reach them easily with minimum effort.

*A disorganized office*  *An organized office*

In some factories, it has been observed that workers walk along the paths which have been used for trolleys which transport raw materials. This is a very unsatisfactory situation in the sense of productivity improvement. Walking on the paths dedicated for trolleys is dangerous and it leads to accidents as well as the destruction of raw materials. It gives twofold damage to the organization. On the one hand, the organization has to spend money to pay compensation for workers, and on the other hand the company loses money due to the wastage caused. So providing separate paths for trolleys and workers is a productive way to minimize accidents as well as wastage of resources.

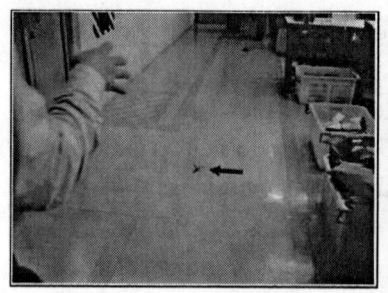

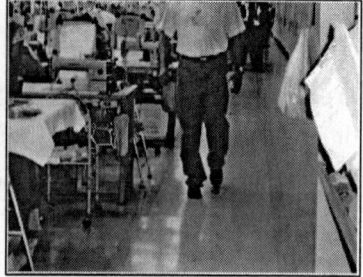

*Paths have been marked clearly*

## 7.5. Motivation of employees

The four factors we already discussed are some physical arrangements in order to reach higher productivity levels. Improved physical arrangements do not give productive results without a motivated workforce. Motivation is the most important factor which managers have to take seriously into consideration to improve productivity in any organization.

Motivation is a kind of stimulating of workers' mental focus to work productively by introducing various kinds of initiatives. In order to motivate workers, monetary provisions (money) or other tangible benefits can be used as one method. However, money is not the only factor to motivate people. There are so many attractive methods to motivate employees other than money. However, providing bonuses, financial rewards for excellent jobs, increased entitlement, extended leave time, etc., are some methods by which people can be motivated financially.

Creating a teamwork environment, sound communication, linkages between employees and employers, appraisal letters, and providing special training for committed employees are other methods of motivating employees. In addition, arranging trips, providing more welfare facilities and creating a sound work environment are also effective methods of motivating employees.

Some organizations provide more welfare facilities not only for workers but also for their family members.

One garment factory selects the best production line daily and a big toy panda is awarded to the members of that line. So they hang the panda near their line throughout the day and on the next day it goes to another team which shows excellence. So, every worker works hard to win the panda. The ultimate result will be higher production and higher productivity.

## 7.6. Quality of the workforce

All members, including management, supervisory and shop floor level workers belong to the workforce and the quality of the workforce directly affects the productivity levels of the organization. Therefore, it is a must to maintain a high quality workforce in order to achieve higher productivity levels. In order to create a quality workforce, there are three areas which should be taken into consideration by the management. Knowledge improvement, skill development and attitude development are these three. These should be maintained or provided at equal levels. If one segment is weaker, it acts as the control factor and then productivity may decrease.

### a. Knowledge improvement

Every employee should have adequate knowledge of his role in order to perform his job. He has to know: what his job is, how it can be done, what the strategies are to perform his job, etc. Hence, management is responsible to educate employees thoroughly. In addition, most management gurus stress that more knowledge development should be done in an organization even though that knowledge may be beyond the requirement of the job which workers have to do. By providing such knowledge, workers have the opportunity to go up the promotional ladder.

**b. Skill development**

Having knowledge about something is not adequate to perform a task productively. Employees should know the ways to perform the job practically. Skill development is needed to do any activity properly and the speed of the task can be increased by improving skills. So, output increases gradually when skills are developed. Lack of skills leads to slow and low output and defective items. Thus, skills development is a must in an organization.

**c. Attitude development**

Attitude development and inculcating positive attitudes in workers' minds is another important step to reach higher productivity levels. Knowledge and skills alone do not give best results without positive attitudes.

For example, driving knowledge can be provided in a classroom. Knowledge on road signs, maintenance of a vehicle and being a good driver can be given in a classroom. However, a person who has good knowledge on all topics relating to driving does not have the ability to drive on the road. So, driving should be practiced extensively with an instructor. That is the way of gaining driving skills.

Nevertheless, any person who has knowledge and skills on driving cannot be considered as a good driver. He should be well-disciplined and should obey the road regulations and signals, respect other drivers as well as pedestrians. These qualities develop as a result of positive attitudes.

Therefore, in order to perform any job productively, one should be equipped with knowledge, skills and positive attitudes. Many people have knowledge and skills but positive attitudes are less common. The contribution of such people is much less to the development of a country. Everyone's responsibility is to contribute to the country's GDP which leads to an economically viable country or an organization.

# CHAPTER 8

# Various Methodologies to be used to improve Productivity

In earlier chapters, different areas on which to focus in order to transform any organization as a productive organization were discussed. There are so many commonly accepted methods/steps which are used in most countries to improve productivity. Some of them are very popular and can be applied in any organization while others can be applied in specific situations. A few of the most common methods are discussed briefly here.

**8.1. Inculcating positive attitudes.**

All employees in an organization should be motivated and focused to achieve the vision, mission and expected goals in the organization. The minds of employees should be attuned in order to create cohesiveness to act as team players, and to participate in results-oriented activities. In addition, workers should plan their jobs or tasks productively and the tasks in the workplace should not conflict or mix with their personal objectives. Hence, strong positive changes created in employees' minds lead to productivity improvement. Therefore, different measures should be taken to create positive attitudes in workers' minds by management. If this is neglected, workers will act negatively and it will be harmful to the organization as well as the personal careers of the employees.

## 8.2. Implementation of 5S concept

5S is a very simple concept which was initiated and implemented in Japanese organizations to improve productivity. Although it is a simple and easy concept, it gives tremendous results. In western countries, this concept is also called housekeeping. This concept will be discussed in detail later.

## 8.3. Suggestion schemes

Suggestion schemes are another method to be introduced in organizations to improve productivity. Under this scheme, all employees are allowed to submit their innovative ideas which generate in their minds, to improve the processes or systems in the organization. The best suggestions are implemented and the employees who authored them are rewarded. Normally, a suggestion box is kept in a specific prominent place in the organization and monthly all suggestions are reviewed and the best suggestions can be selected. This method encourages employees to think innovatively and contribute to the success of the organization. Suggestion schemes encourage workers who do not like to talk publicly or who do not have direct access to top management.

## 8.4. Quality Circles

In an organization, different kinds of small voluntary teams can be formed to perform its tasks effectively and efficiently. These teams may be based on production lines, specific activities or sections. The team members get together and discuss ways and means to improve the productivity of their tasks as well as any shortcomings. Then they voluntarily discuss the remedies to be taken to rectify these issues. Later these solutions are submitted to the management and the best alternative solutions are implemented with the blessing of the top management.

The main point behind the quality circles is participation of both operational and supervisory levels because the workers in these levels have a better understanding of the work processes than the top management as they are the people who really engage in the work. The proposals or solutions from different quality circles which are submitted to the top management act as a pool of good proposals to management to be implemented for the success of the organization. By doing so, workers also feel that their proposals were considered. and the organization belongs to them. This kind of feeling is called "sense of ownership" or "sense of belongingness". A sense of ownership is a strong factor that contributes to the sustainable development of the organization. However, there are some technical guidelines and quality circle tools which are to be used and studied in order to implement quality circles. Before going for quality circles, a proper knowledge on these tools is essential. It should be emphasised that forming groups and talking without using quality circle techniques or tools cannot be considered as implementation of quality circles.

## 8.5. Eliminating waste

A major method that Japan uses is the elimination of waste. Japan believes that minimization of waste is easier than earning money by increasing the price of a product or a service. Wastage can be simply divided into two types, namely, the wastage occurring due to negligence and the wastage occurring without knowing that it is wastage. Wastage due to negligence means allowing resources to be wasted even though you can observe it. Such kind of wastage can be prevented easily if needed.

Wastage caused without any knowledge of it, means that it cannot be identified easily. If a process is observed very carefully, such type of wastage can be identified. For example, an incident occurred in Sri Lanka in 2002. Due to the lack of space in the record room in one organization, it was decided to find a new location which had 1000 sq. feet of space to store additional documents. Therefore, one staff officer was instructed by his superior to find a place immediately. The staff officer first analyzed this situation and applied the 5S concept into the existing record room. All unnecessary documents were removed from the record room and ultimately that officer was able to free ¼ of the record room. The officer asserted that the same record room could be used for another three years. If that officer had found a new location, as instructed by the top officer, the organization would have had to pay a large sum of money as the rent. In 2002, the cost of one square foot in Colombo city was LKR 40 per month. If a place with a space of 1000 sq-feet was rented, LKR 40,000 per month would have to be paid. The cost for a 3-year period would be LKR 1.4m (Approximately USD 14,000). If that staff officer hadn't analyzed this carefully, 1.4m would have to be paid yet. Because of implementation of 5S, it was avoided. This was a result of careful analysis of waste minimization. (Note that such types of officers should be rewarded and commended.)

However, any kind of waste should be eliminated and this leads to productivity improvement. The only way to eliminate wastage is to have sound knowledge of ways which prevent wastage and the productivity improvement concepts.

In Japan, based on the nature of the wastage, it is divided into three categories, namely as muda, mura and muri. Even though it is divided into three, all fall under the wastage.

### 8.5.1. Muda

Any activity has two aspects. One is value added activity and other is non-value added activity. As far as productivity is concerned, non value added activities do not make any contribution to productivity improvement other than it adds cost to the product or a service. So value added activities are always encouraged in a process. If there are non-value added activities in a process, which cannot be removed, they should be controlled as much as possible. So the waste caused by any non-value added activity is called muda. Under muda seven types of wastes are discussed. They are also called the "Seven Sins" in Japan because wastage creates only damages to anyone or anyplace. Let's discuss these seven types of wastes briefly.

#### 8.5.1.1. Over-production

If any kind of product or a service is produced beyond the expected or required demand, the excess would be wastage of resources and it adversely affects the productivity of the organization. If over production occurs, material, manpower, money and time may be wasted and such over production may not get to the real market. The future market cannot also be predicted for long periods. So everything could be wasted.

For example, if a soap factory produces more soap than required consumption, it can be treated as wastage. Someone can argue that it is not wastage because the excess can be stored and taken for use later. In order to store excess amounts of production, there must be enough space. Extra space means extra cost. In order to maintain stores unnecessarily, any organization has to spend money and labour. It is unnecessary administrative cost and wastage. Hence, maintaining excess stock due to overproduction causes wastage and minimizes productivity. (However, in stock control systems, it is advised to maintain a buffer stock. Maintaining a buffer stock is essential. Waste minimization does not mean removing buffer stocks. Therefore, the concept of waste elimination should not be confused with the concept of maintaining buffer stocks).

### 8.5.1.2. Waiting for materials and operations

Any process needs materials. In order to maintain the process productively, materials should be provided in a timely fashion. Otherwise operators have to wait until materials arrive. This is wastage of time and during this time, workers as well as machines are idle. So it is an increase of idling time.

Furthermore, if any activity or an operation consumes more time than the stipulated time for that activity, it is wastage also. After all, time is money. If time can be used as productively as possible, it leads to high productivity levels. Normally, factories are located in the areas in which raw materials are available because it minimizes the transportation time. As a result, waiting time also can be minimized.

### 8.5.1.3. Unnecessary transportation.

Any manufacturing process or a service may require some transport such as material transporting, document transporting, etc. Any transport which does not add value to the product is wastage. Therefore, the transporting should be minimized in order to reduce such wastage.

In offices, files have to be transferred from place to place, from one officer to another officer. The time taken to transfer the file can also be treated as a form of transportation. If the time taken to transfer that file increases, the transportation time also increases. If a file has to be transported unnecessarily it consumes more time that will also be an unnecessary transport. In order to minimize such unnecessary transport, the work setup should be planned well and then time and labour can be minimized.

### 8.5.1.4. Unnecessary Operations / processes

If you study a process very carefully, you will be able to identify some unnecessary operations or work steps. Such unnecessary operations consume more resources and they are wastage. Through work studies, unnecessary operations can be identified and then such operations can be eliminated. This will minimize resources required such as money, material, labour and time.

I had an opportunity to conduct a work study in a government office in 1991 for a thesis which had to be submitted for my higher studies. I studied all the steps of the main process of completing the specific task in that office. I found that there were a few steps which could be easily removed from the process. The management of the office also studied my report and removed steps identified by me and the ultimate result was that the time taken for the whole process could be reduced by two hours.

It is clearly understood that any steps which can be easily removed from a process do not make any contribution to the value of the activity. Hence, such steps are called non value added activities (NVA). Therefore, anyone who is concerned about improving productivity should be able to identify non value added steps in processes in any work environment. It is a very fruitful way of eliminating waste.

## 8.5.1.5. Unnecessary inventory

As a result of overproduction, the size of inventories goes up and creates an extra burden to all including shipping, stores and management departments. It also duplicates the work. Unnecessary inventory means consuming more space and creating extra costs. So maintenance cost goes up. Time has to be wasted to keep records unnecessarily. Extra personnel have to be employed. Minimizing overproduction and the following "Just in Time" (JIT) rule is the best solution for getting rid of unnecessary inventories. As a result of unnecessary inventory, unnecessary documents are also to be maintained. Traditional management used to keep more documents and often the same documents are recorded and stored in different places unnecessarily. This is not only duplicating the work but also consuming more space for storing such documents. However, more sophisticated methods, such as the proper application of Information Technology (IT) can minimize unnecessary documents. This is the best way to minimize paper documents and it reduces the use of paper as well as the utilization of space.

## 8.5.1.6. Unnecessary Motions

As well as unnecessary operations, unnecessary motions also create waste. As discussed in earlier chapters, if the distance between a clerk and his file cabinet is abnormally large, the clerk has to walk too far and it does not contribute to the value of the process. If this distance can be reduced as much as possible, the service of the clerk can be optimized.

Locating executive officers and lower grade officers in remote places causes such type of unnecessary movements. Consequently, by locating the staff in appropriate locations after proper work studies, the productivity of such processes can be optimized, leading to overall productivity improvement of the whole process.

For another example, if printers have been connected to a network and all computer terminals have been connected to those printers, then all operators on computer terminals can share the printers. So networking printers is a good concept to utilize resources productively and then the cost of equipment can be minimized. However, this should be seriously and carefully considered because it also should be feasible and practical. If all operators have to walk too much distance to collect the printouts and if they have to wait to collect printouts, it causes unnecessary motions and delays. Therefore, enough printers should be installed in the network in appropriate locations in order to reduce unnecessary motions and delays. Otherwise, the reduction of the cost by networking printers may be lower than the wastage caused by unnecessary motions and the expected productivity levels cannot be achieved.

Furthermore, all equipment in factories should also be located according to this theory. The machines should also be designed according to this rule and the body movement of workers should be taken into consideration. By doing so, workers can operate machines with less effort which minimizes fatigue. Therefore, giving much attention to ergonomics in work places reduces unnecessary motions of workers and fatigue. It also will reduce wastage.

A sound work setup minimizes unnecessary motions and increases the productivity level of the system.

*A proper work set up to reduce motions*

### 8.5.1.7. Rejects or refused goods or services

If the end product or result of any process falls under the reject category even before it goes to the customer or even after it was purchased by the customer, it is also considered as wastage. If rejects come out from the production line, they have to be sent to be reworked. It is a duplication of work which may double not only the cost but also stress. If defective or low quality products are released to the market, they cannot be sold at the real price marked. Therefore, the income received will be lesser than expected income because such defective items have to be sold at reduced prices. For example, when you purchase a dress, you are very careful about it and examine it thoroughly. If slight damage is observed, you never pay the marked price and refrain from buying it or try to reduce the price.

When you buy, even a loaf of bread, you are very concerned about the weight and the quality of it. If it is over baked or under baked or with any defects no one buys it. If all loaves of bread are baked in such a manner the customers will select another bakery or place to buy bread. The ultimate result would be the closing down of the bakery which produces defective bread. It means that unsuccessful organizations cannot survive in a competitive market. Although the product or service is defective or not, the same amount of resources consumes in the production process. It means that the amount of inputs used do not generate the real value of output. As we know it is low productivity.

This argument can equally be applied to services also. If the service is not accepted by the customer or the customer criticizes the service, this type of service can also be considered as a defective product/service. Any service should be delivered at least to meet the customer expectations. However, productive organizations have passed that limitation and they have moved from meeting customer expectations to customer delight. It means they provide more service than the customer expected.

For example, a receptionist should deliver service well enough to satisfy the visitors and it is very important because reception is the place the first impression is created. Cordial acceptance, a friendly smile, attractive attire, and cheerful speaking are a few of the best strategies to attract customers by creating a good impression in the customer's mind. This type of behaviour is appreciated by customers and it helps to sustain the customers forever as well as to have more loyalty to the organization. By having such strategies any organization can maintain a good, strong first impression. It has been shown that any organization has to spend five times the money to find a new customer rather than retaining an existing customer.

If the behaviour of the receptionist is negative and unattractive, customers will be unimpressed with the service and start criticizing it. This is the starting point of losing customers and collapsing any organization.

By taking all these facts into consideration, we can understand that any product should be produced and released to the market without any defects and such products should be according to customer expectations. Likewise any service should also be delivered to meet customer expectations. It is a great responsibility of the management to conduct regular studies and introduce improvements to the system and processes to cater the customers to satisfy and retain them.

Note:- Some productivity and quality practitioners mention "unused employee knowledge or creativity" as the eighth waste. However, 7 wastes which were discussed earlier are tangible and measurable. Unused knowledge or creativity is intangible and immeasurable. If any organization can make use of their employees' creativity it would be a great asset in productivity achievement journey in any organization.

### 8.5.2. Mura

Mura means unevenness, inconsistence, and irregularity. If work flow is not even, there is mura. For example, consider a production line. All members in the line should be equally speedy. Otherwise the speed is limited by the slowest person. Then others' labour is wasted. So, necessary precautions should be taken to reduce unevenness.

### 8.5.3 Muri

Muri means overburden. For example, suppose a bus is overloaded. It creates damages to the bus quickly. It is a loss. Such type of waste is muri. If an employee is given a heavy work load which he cannot perform, then muri happens. As a result of muri, the probability to produce low quality, defective items goes up. Then it can be treated as muda also.

Now it is understood that mura and muri also creates muda. The following pictures give more understanding on muda, mura and muri.

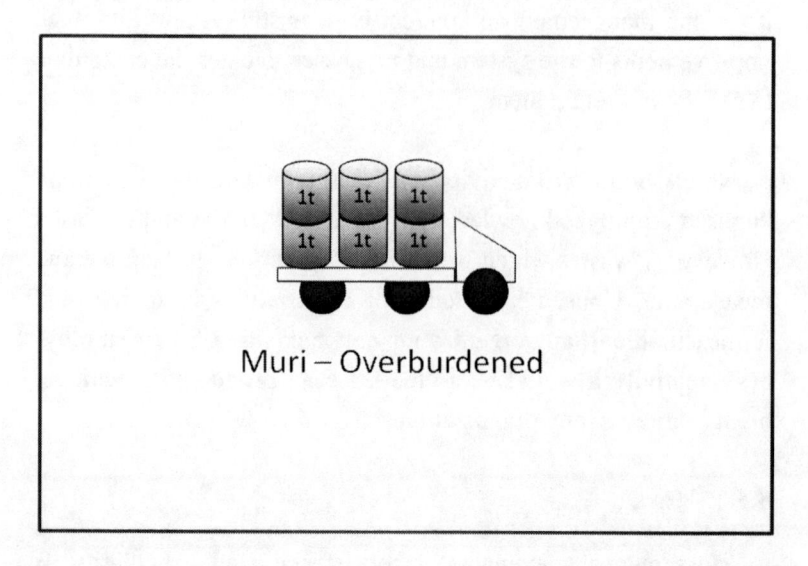

Muri – Overburdened

**Mura – Unevenness, fluctuation or variation**

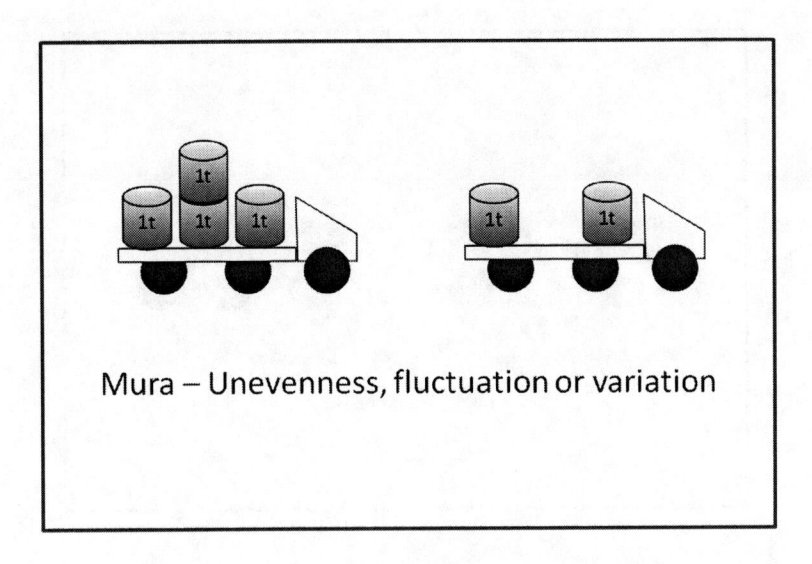

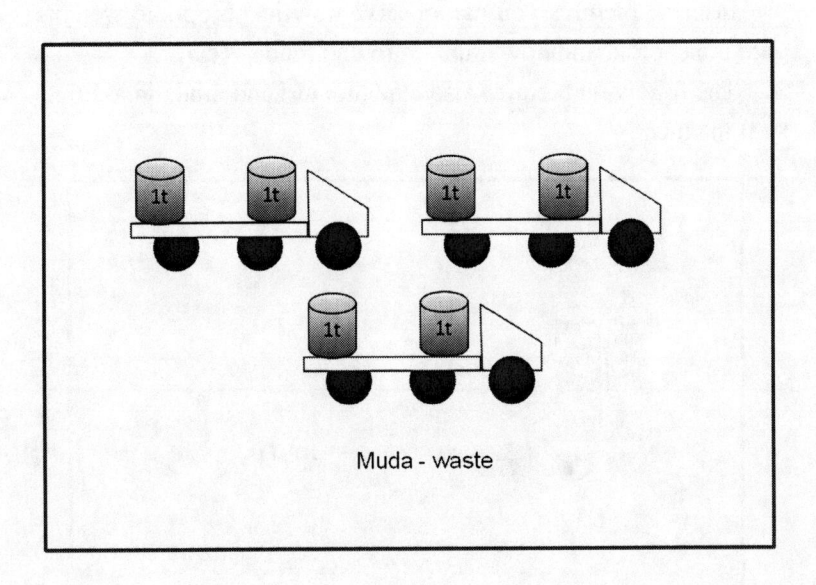

**Muda - waste**

[Figure: Two trucks each carrying 3×1t barrels. Caption: "No muda, No mura, No muri"]

In these pictures you can observe how inappropriate weights are transported and how mura, muri and muda occur.

The following pictures also explain muri and muda in a different manner.

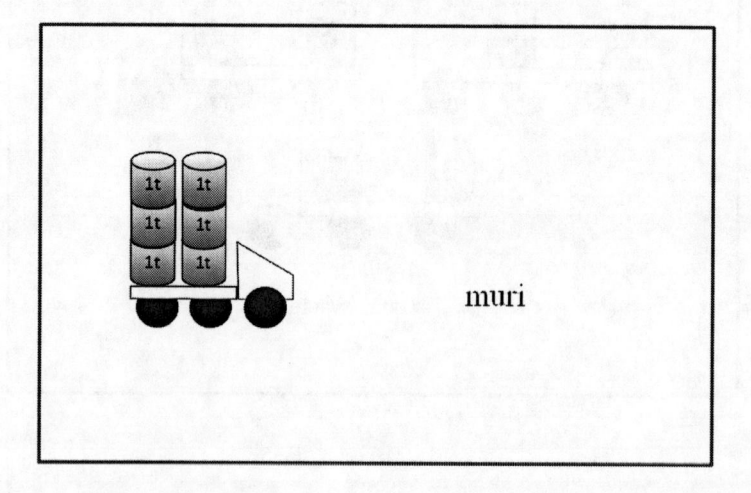

[Figure: Truck overloaded with 6×1t barrels stacked. Label: "muri"]

muda

## 8.6. Q.C.D. Concept

This concept explains the importance of quality, cost and delivery. In earlier chapters the importance of quality and cost was discussed. It is vital to optimize the quality of a product or a service in order to achieve higher productivity levels. In addition, the importance of minimizing the cost of inputs was discussed. However, it is not adequate to produce higher quality goods or services with a minimum cost in order to achieve higher productivity levels. The product or service should be delivered to the customer when the customer wants it. It is called "in time" delivery.

For example, pizza delivery is a very well-known service everywhere. If pizza cannot be delivered to the customer at the expected time, there is no use in maintaining high quality or minimizing the cost of production. If the end user cannot make use of it, it becomes a rejected item. So, the in time delivery is very important as well as maintaining quality and minimizing cost of production.

If pension benefits can be granted to an officer at the time he retires, it can be treated as an in time delivery of a service. If providing pension benefits is delayed, the pensioner is not satisfied with the service even though quality service is provided with a minimum cost. Therefore, the Q.C.D concept can be applied in every organization in order to achieve higher levels of productivity improvements.

## 8.7. Implementation of "Kaizen"

"Kaizen" is a Japanese word which denotes continuous improvement. Most Japanese organizations have succeeded by introducing "Kaizen" in their organizations. The main feature of this concept is introducing very small changes slowly, step by step, rather than introducing massive breakthroughs. This is done by adding a new feature to a product or a service to increase the effectiveness and efficiency, improve the attractiveness, etc.

For example, compare the difference between a radio produced in the 1970s and a modern radio. How many new features have been added to the old radio to convert it into today's one? These changes were done step by step. By changing the technological specifications, a lot of products have been introduced to the market. This is a continuous process and in the future we will be able to use more sophisticated products than today.

An old radio       A new radio

In addition, compare a motor car in the 1970s and today. The Japanese introduced more new features and current motor cars are vastly different from the cars produced in the 1970s. DVD players, air conditioners, automatic transmissions, power doors and locks, power mirrors, power windows, air bags, etc. have been added to introduce more customer pleasing cars to the market. All these changes are due to the "Kaizen" approach. So it is very clearly understood that many items we consume today have been subject to the "Kaizen" approach.

*An old car*       *A new car*

The "Kaizen" approach goes with innovative ideas. Hence, creativity and innovativeness are the main factors which contributed to the "Kaizen" approach.

The following picture is a garage used to park vehicles. You can observe that more than 2 vehicles cannot be parked in the garage. In Japan, an innovation has been made to park 35 vehicles using the same space.

The mechanism of the ferris wheel has been used to develop this new method.

*Picture of a ferris wheel*

The ferris wheel is circular. In this new innovation, the shape has been changed to an oval shape. Each compartment of the ferris wheel has been designed as a parking space. This sketch diagram shows the structure of this system

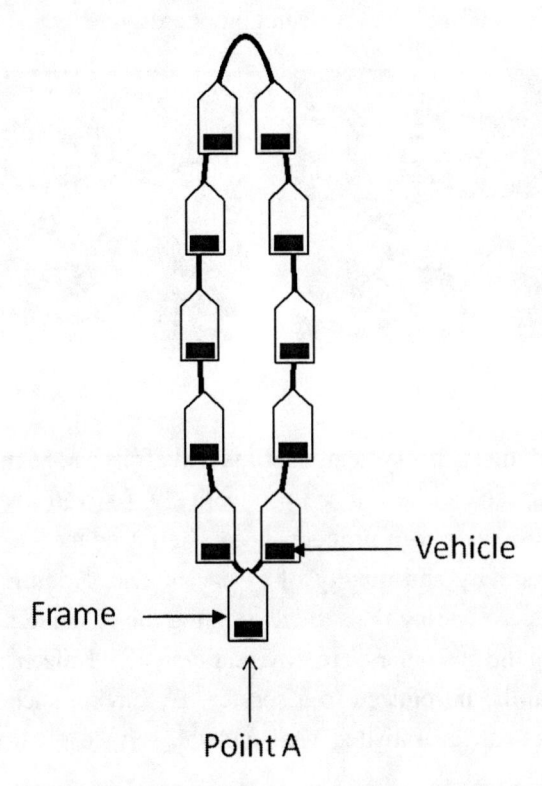

*(Diagram: oval ferris wheel structure with compartments labeled "Vehicle", central "Frame", and "Point A" at the bottom)*

This wheel can be rotated and vehicles enter at point A. When the vehicle is parked, the wheel is rotated and a new empty compartment arrives at point A. In this manner, 35 vehicles can be parked using this structure.

When the owner wants to take out his car, he has to provide the number of the compartment in which his car was parked, to the caretaker. The caretaker rotates the wheel and takes the respective compartment to point A and the owner can remove the vehicle.

As the space is very limited in this structure, turning the car is also difficult. Consequently, the car is reversed onto a plate that is located in front of the garage which can be rotated. The plate is rotated by 180° and then car can go out easily.

*Car rotates*        *Car goes*

By having such a system, the time and effort can be minimized and the space can be utilized productively. As well as "Kaizen" being introduced to a product, it can be introduced to improve the productivity and quality of a service also. Adding different features to delivering the service, treating the customers well and satisfying the customers, are different types of "Kaizen" methods which can be introduced to a service. By having such systems, customers can be satisfied well and the service quality can be optimized.

When the customers visit the organization to obtain the service, cordial acceptance is a must. In addition, comfortable seating arrangements for customers can be supplied. The environment can be arranged attractively. The response time can be minimized as much as possible. In order to create a sound background, "Kaizen" innovations can be introduced to the steps of any process. By converting the organizations into productive places, the customers as well as the employees will be satisfied.

*Police station- Kirulapona, Sri Lanka*

## 8.8. Application of Information Technology (ICT)

Currently information technology has encroached everywhere irrespectively whether it is a production or service sector. It also has made marvellous changes to every process or system. Introducing ICT reduces the time, cost and labour while it increases the efficiency and effectiveness of any process. Finally, it reduces the input cost and it increases productivity. Therefore, heads of organizations should take every action to promote ICT in their organizations. Training employees, purchasing appropriate instruments and encouraging employees to use them are main responsibilities of managers in the process of ICT development in their organizations.

As a country, policy makers should make policy changes in order to enable everyone to use ICT everywhere. Tax concessions, providing more opportunities for IT education and establishing more institutions for IT education are some of the basic things which a government can do.

## 8.9. Knowledge Management

Simply, knowledge management is creating, sharing and applying knowledge to enhance the productivity of any organization. It can be implemented with the participation of all members in any organization without any barriers. People have two kinds of knowledge. They are tacit knowledge and implicit knowledge.

Tacit knowledge is that knowledge which a person has but cannot be articulated. It is difficult to transfer to others. Implicit knowledge can be transferred easily. However, if someone needs to, he can follow some methods to translate tacit knowledge to implicit knowledge.

However, knowledge sharing and transferring is a vital factor to create innovative things. So it should be encouraged by any head of the organization.

## 8.10. Balanced Scorecard

The Balanced Scorecard is another productivity improvement tool. However, it is mostly for the managerial level. It is used for planning as well as monitoring. Four perspectives, namely, financial perspective, customer perspective, learning & growth perspective, and internal process perspective are analysed under the Balanced Scorecard and accordingly, managers should take action to drive the organization towards the correct destination. It is a very good tool for managers to determine whether the organization is running smoothly and productively by identifying key result areas and key performance indicators. They can make adjustments according to the changes in each perspective using key performance indicators of each perspective.

## 8.11. Total Quality Management

Quality is the most important word from the point of view of the customer as well as the producer. If the producer produces goods with low quality, he cannot sell such items at the real price in the market. Customers also never buy such items as the low quality products bring troubles to the customer. Therefore, the quality of the end product or a service is the most significant feature. In order to have the end product at high quality, each step of the process should be under quality control. Quality of the material, machines, and people is very vital to control the quality of the process. Maintaining the quality in every aspect is called total quality management. In order to have quality management, the management level has to take different kind of steps including implementation of productivity and quality concepts in the organizations.

## 8.12. Six Sigma

Six sigma is another advance productivity tool which every organization should implement. It brings remarkable benefits to the organization. The concept behind this in simply is minimizing defects up to certain accepted level. If the defect opportunities of a product or a service can be brought down to six sigma level which is 3.4 parts per million/3.4 opportunities per million (3.4ppm), it is considered that the product or service has reached to six sigma level. You should be able to understand that how many steps and precautions should be taken to reach such type of level. However, there are lot of popular companies in the world which have already brought their products up to six sigma level.

Therefore, every head of the organization should set their goals keeping six sigma in their minds also.

We discussed different methods which can be applied to improve the productivity in any organization. In addition to them there are more methods that can be applied. Some of them are ISO certification, Just in Time (JIT) and business process re-engineering. As the main intention of this book is introducing productivity and 5S, more details are not discussed on such topics.

# CHAPTER 9

## 5S Concept

5S is a very simple concept which gives remarkable benefits, developed in Japan and it has been popularized in other countries during the past few decades. It is a concept which should be studied and practiced in every home, every office, every workplace and every school and by every citizen in order to reach higher productivity levels. 5S is a basic concept which can be applied by everyone everywhere in order to improve quality and productivity. However, the speed of popularizing this concept is still not satisfactory because of the lack of clear understanding of this concept among the average public and the lack of a proper mechanism to introduce it to others in most countries.

It is very important to discuss the reasons for giving priority to the 5S concept in the productivity promotion campaign although there are so many other tools available to improve productivity. Let's consider the main reasons why the 5S concept should be introduced and implemented in organizations to improve productivity.

## 9.1. Reasons for introducing the 5S concept

### 9.1.1. It is very easy to implement it in any place.

In order to implement this concept, less effort is required. So it is very easy to implement 5S anywhere. Implementation of 5S is not a stressful task. It is joyful.

### 9.1.2. Anyone can understand easily.

As this is a very simple concept, any person can understand easily. Even a small child can study and understand this concept. For example, by familiarizing this concept among children, they can be oriented to keep their belongings, including their books, clothes and shoes properly in specific locations. Housewives can arrange and maintain the home and kitchen in an orderly and attractive manner and it will help them to work without any disturbances. Furthermore, employees can maintain their workplace properly.

### 9.1.3. This concept can be applied to any place

It is very easy to apply this concept everywhere including offices, schools, hospitals, post offices, factories and even at home.

### 9.1.4. The cost of implementation is very low

The cost of implementation of this concept is very low. There are so many low cost practices which can be introduced under this concept. Hence, even an organization which is not financially sound can easily implement this. Any person also can implement this concept without much cost. However, the advantages and profits of implementation of this concept are tremendous.

### 9.1.5. 5S is the foundation step of productivity improvement

Productivity improvement is a never-ending journey in any organization. As the starting point, 5S should be implemented in order to make a strong sustainable foundation for the productivity improvement of the organization. Without implementing 5S, it is very difficult to introduce other advanced productivity tools which were discussed in a previous chapter.

5S denotes five Japanese words namely, Seiri, Seiton, Seiso, Seiketsu and Shitsuke. Since all words start from the letter "S", it is called "5S". As we discussed earlier, this concept was initiated and implemented in Japan. It can be summarized as an incredible concept which laid the foundation for reaching higher productivity levels in Japan. It was a blessing for Japan which had collapsed economically as well as physically after the Second World War. In western countries, these 5 Japanese words have been translated as, sorting, set in order, shining, standardization and sustaining.

During the past few decades, developing countries learned this strategy and implemented it in their respective countries and achieved very favourable results. Currently most developed countries in the Asia Pacific region have gone further and introduced other productivity concepts as Japan did. Most companies in the USA also used the slogan, "If Japan can, why can't we?" to encourage employees in their organizations to make them productive. Singapore, Malaysia, South Korea, and Taiwan are just a few countries which gained tremendous results by implementing the 5S concept.

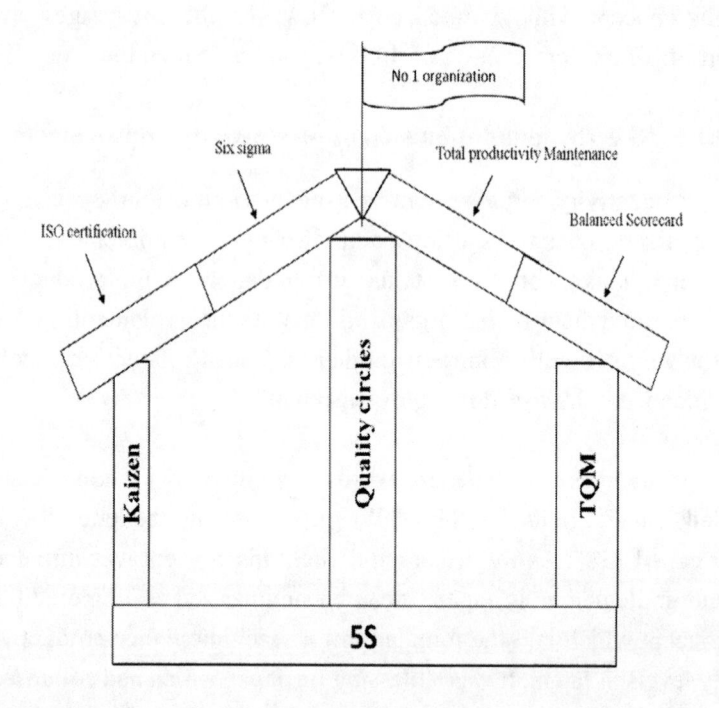

```
                    No 1 organization
                         |
         Six sigma       |      Total productivity Maintenance
                    \    |    /
    ISO certification \  |  /   Balanced Scorecard
              \        \ | /        /
                         ^
                    /    |    \
                   /     |     \
      Kaizen    Quality circles    TQM
                         
                        5S
```

In addition, the labour management cooperation in Japan is very strong. 5S also strengthens labour relations. So workers know their roles well and they always try to do their jobs optimally. This concept has been inculcated in their minds. After introducing and implementing 5S, it is very easy to align the minds of employees towards productive output. Thus, they work productively, earn more and enjoy their lives well. Therefore, the impact of implementation of 5S has many successful aspects.

The implementation of 5S means the application of very simple steps: arranging the workplace properly, keeping and maintaining it neatly, and introducing some improvements are the few steps which have to be implemented.

This concept has been applied in factories as well as in public organizations in Japan and it has shown remarkable positive changes. It has also facilitated the administration. It has been implemented at the household level also. In order to make everyone aware of this concept, it has been included in the educational system in Japan. As a result, the Japanese have been able to manage their lives well when compared to citizens in other countries in the Asia Pacific region.

## 9.2. Benefits of implementation of 5S

When 5S was introduced in Japan, the Japanese understood that there were many advantages in it. Let's discuss them one by one.

### 9.2.1. Ability to gain employee participation in management

It is a fact that employee participation is an essential factor in modern management. It has been understood that top down management and bottom up management are not the best methods to run organizations. Therefore, 5S is a strong bridge to link management and the workers' level and reduces the gap between them. When this link is strong, employees' good ideas for the development of the organization including products and services can be easily obtained. This type of environment will facilitate for moving suggestion schemes and implementation of quality circles.

### 9.2.2. It encourages teamwork and team effort brings more results than individual work deployment

If any task is performed individually, more effort has to be put out. If that same task is done by two people, the job gets easier. This is called the "synergetic effect". It means 1+1 is not equal to "2" but it is more than "2". It may be 3 or 4 or so on depending on the nature of the team. When a task is performed by one person, the productivity may be less. If more people join to do the same task, it will be more productive. Therefore, all the employees in an organization should work as a team in order to get higher results. 5S creates an environment for people to work as a team in the organization.

### 9.2.3. 5S creates an overall basic background in an organization to make it productive

The initial stage of any activity should have a successful foundation. It creates a productive mindset and the minds of the people in the organization are aligned toward to common goals of the organization. Therefore, everyone tries to do the job productively. In order to facilitate this smooth running, all initial steps have to be initiated successfully. If 5S is in practice in an organization, it is easier to start any development activity, than for any organization where 5S is not practiced.

### 9.2.4. 5S improves safety in any workplace

Occupational health and safety should be given the first priority in the workplace. Now, adherence to safety standards in the workplace has been regularised in most of the countries in order to minimize the accident rate. That's why the "Safety First" concept is understood in workplace. The implementation of 5S reduces the risks of accidents everywhere. After implementation of 5S any place gets an orderly arranged workplace. The reasons for most of accidents are disorganized, dirty, workplace environments. 5S removes all such barriers. Finally the probability of accidents occurring will drop drastically because of the implementation of 5S. Then workers will work happily without any fear. This concept applies not only to the workplace but also to school, home, kitchen garden, etc.

### 9.2.5. Increases the morale of the employees

In an environment which is free from accidents, hazards, and fear, employees will be happy. When the employees get opportunities to work and communicate with the management they will be happier. Ultimately, it automatically creates high morale among employees. Improving morale cannot be created by paying more wages, incentives or any other physical benefits. It also cannot be created by force. It should come out from minds of the employees automatically. What managers can do to generate morale is make a sound environment in which to work. 5S will do this job on behalf of managers. So what managers can do is encourage everyone in the workplace to go for implementation of 5S. In addition, implementation of 5S increases the pride of workmanship in an organization. It also leads to quality products and services.

### 9.2.6. Improves visible control.

Most of the improvements done under 5S are through visible signs, labels and colours. When something goes wrong or not according to the standards set, anyone can notice it very easily and quickly. If anyone cannot notice some harmful incident or sign, it may cause severe damages. As 5S is a visible control method, it can be noticed and remedial action can be taken quickly. So it prevents heavy losses to the organization. It leads to reduce down time also. If down time is long, it may affect production volume. It is also a loss to the organization.

### 9.2.7. Reduces breakdowns

Most breakdowns are because of poor maintenance of the instruments. Accumulated dirty particles accelerate the breakdowns. Because of dirt, it is impossible to notice small oil leaks, loose parts which create cracks and vibrations in machines. Long term prevalence of such minor faults create major damages to the machines which causes long down times and requires more money to get them repaired. Implementation of 5S removes all dirt and unnecessary debris. So machines and instruments are always clean. Even minor damage can also be observed easily.

### 9.2.8. Leads to increase the quality of processes as well as products

When working environment and machines are maintained in a quality manner (Total Productivity Maintenance) and the morale of workers is high, quality products or services would be the final output. It means high sales and high profits. That is the ultimate objective of any organization.

### 9.2.9. It empowers employees

As 5S is a collective effort, everyone should participate in implementation of it. More suggestions from employees should also come out. The implementers should also be the employees. So employees also have a power to contribute to the smooth running of the organization. Under the 5S implementation, some decisions are taken by the employees. So the employees are compelled to sustain these systems and developments created by them because they did not originated from a top down approach. Employees feel a sense of ownership of their developments.

### 9.2.10. 5S saves money

If the workplace is arranged properly, everyone can work easily with less effort, less time, fewer accidents, fewer steps and so on. This means less cost. The cost reduction by implementing 5S has been proved by a large number of organizations.

Taking all these benefits into consideration, we can understand that the 5S concept is very helpful in any place. Hence, it is important to study the principles behind the 5S concept. However, studying 5S is not adequate. Implementation is also essential. Finally, it has to be taught to everyone by any means such as books, articles, words of mouth, etc. Therefore, your responsibility is to learn 5S, implement 5S, teach others and encourage them to implement it. The concept of 5S is discussed in the next chapters.

# CHAPTER 10

## Seiri-Sorting and Organization

The first step of 5S is Seiri. First, necessary and unnecessary things are segregated into two parts and unnecessary things are removed. At this point, a problem arises in defining unnecessary things and removing them. Somebody can say that it is necessary while others say that it is not necessary. Such situation creates problems among 5S implementers. So the red tag system is followed to decide whether an item is necessary or not.

Under the red tag procedure, any item which any member in the 5S process feels is not necessary is moved to a specific designated area called the red tag area. This area should also be labelled as "Red Tag Area". When an item is moved to the red tag area, it should be tagged with a red tag. The red tag is red in colour and it includes a description of the item moved to the red tag area. The person, who moves the item, should fill the details in the left side of the red tag tagged with the item. A specimen of a red tag is shown as follows.

## 5S RED TAG

Date............ Tagged by...................

Item description...............................

Department ......................................

| Item Type: | | Action to take: |
|---|---|---|
| ☐ Raw Materials ☐ Finished goods | | ☐ Trash |
| ☐ Tools ☐ Instruments | | ☐ Hold |
| ☐ Equipment ☐ Machine parts | | ☐ Move to .............. |
| ☐ WIP (work in progress) ☐ Other | | ☐ Contact................... |
| Other ......................... | | ☐ Other .................. |

**Reasons Tagged:**

☐ no longer used

☐ Unknown Owner

☐ Doesn't work

☐ Other ........................

**Manager's Initial :-----**

Date:-------------------

Tag No:----------------

At the red tag site, a responsible person inspects the items and decides whether it should be removed, destroyed or sold. Normally this responsible person could be a manager. When the inspection is done he can get others ideas also. He fills the right side of the red tag and put his initials. The main factors considered when determining if items are to be removed, Is this item needed? How often this item is needed? If removed will there be a problem, etc. After completing the details in the red tag, each tag should be given a serial No in order to enter these details in the red tag register for record keeping purposes. Even though the red tag register is in paper format, I like to emphasize that maintaining it in electronic format would reduce paper. Such type of paper documents again start consuming space even in minor scale.

Once finalizing the items to be removed, they are kept aside in the same location for a week and later they are moved to another location called central location and all items lie there for 30 days. During this period anyone can recall an item if needed. After 30 days all these items in the central location are removed.

Before removing unnecessary items, they are segregated into three categories as follows.

1. Items which have no value and can be disposed of easily.
2. Items which have some value.
3. Items which have some value but cannot be disposed of easily.

*Sorting for red tagging in an office*

The following diagram explains the steps to be taken in the process of seiri.

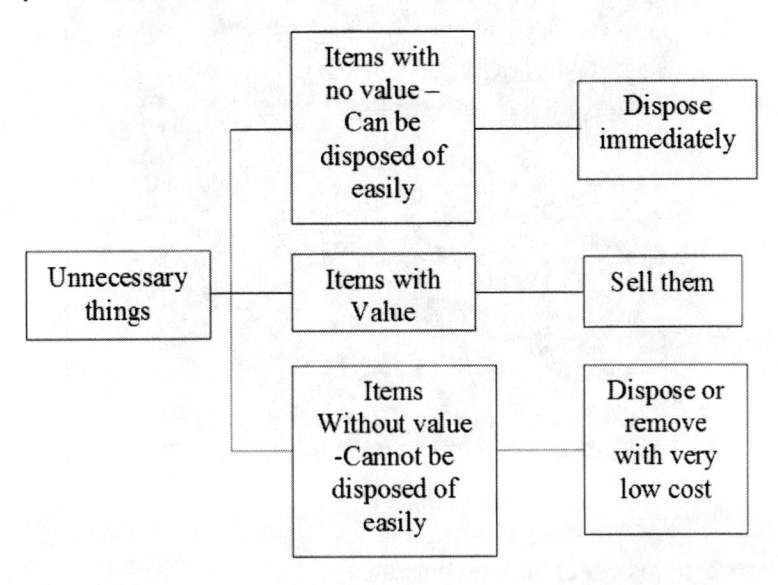

```
                    ┌─────────────┐
                    │ Items with  │
                    │ no value –  │      ┌──────────────┐
                ┌───│ Can be      │──────│   Dispose    │
                │   │ disposed of │      │ immediately  │
                │   │ easily      │      └──────────────┘
                │   └─────────────┘
┌─────────────┐ │   ┌─────────────┐      ┌──────────────┐
│ Unnecessary │─┼───│ Items with  │──────│  Sell them   │
│   things    │ │   │    Value    │      │              │
└─────────────┘ │   └─────────────┘      └──────────────┘
                │   ┌─────────────┐      ┌──────────────┐
                │   │   Items     │      │  Dispose or  │
                │   │ Without     │      │   remove     │
                └───│ value       │──────│  with very   │
                    │ -Cannot be  │      │  low cost    │
                    │ disposed of │      └──────────────┘
                    │ easily      │
                    └─────────────┘
```

These unnecessary items may be present in your workplace, office or home. This process can be applied anywhere. Let's discuss these three steps in detail.

**10.1. Items which have any value and can be disposed of easily**

Such items do not have a value. Old scratched documents, papers, covers, wrappings, etc. fall into this category. Such items can be discarded immediately. Burning and burying are some steps that can be taken to discard such things. However, these things should be disposed using environmentally friendly methods. For example, old paper, plastic, etc can be sent to recycling plants. Some items cannot be burnt because the by-products of burning may be environmentally hazardous. In such instances, recommended methodologies should be adopted to discard such items.

*Items to be destroyed*

## 10.2. Items which have some value

Some unwanted items may have value. Old newspapers, empty bottles, old metal, wood, and cardboard are some examples. Such type of items can be reused or recycled. Therefore, such items can be sold. By selling such items some income can be generated in addition to getting rid of the unnecessary items. Items like used computers and furniture can be given to others who can use them.

## 10.3. Items which have some value but cannot be disposed of easily

Some items don't have a significant value. For example, old files used in an office do not have a value except on some occasions when some information needs to be retrieved. Such items should be stored at a place like a record or archives room and not in the usual office premises. Thus lower cost methods should be used to store such items. When storing of paper documents is done, new technology must be used. A large number of documents which take a big space can be scanned using heavy duty scanners and stored in digital format. It saves a substantial amount of space and money.

By following these three steps, it is very easy to get rid of unwanted things and thereafter, only wanted items remain.

# CHAPTER 11

## Seiton- Arranging and Neatness - (Set in Order)

*Well arranged store*

The second step of 5S is to arrange properly all items identified as wanted in the first step. In order to arrange them properly, a few simple techniques are used. By arranging such items properly even in an office, school, shop, garage or anywhere, the handling of such items will be easier. It saves time. If the setup is improper, it takes more time to retrieve such items.

Saving time means saving money. In addition, proper storing and arranging minimizes waste and increases safety. In this step, wanted items are divided into two groups, namely items used frequently and items used rarely.

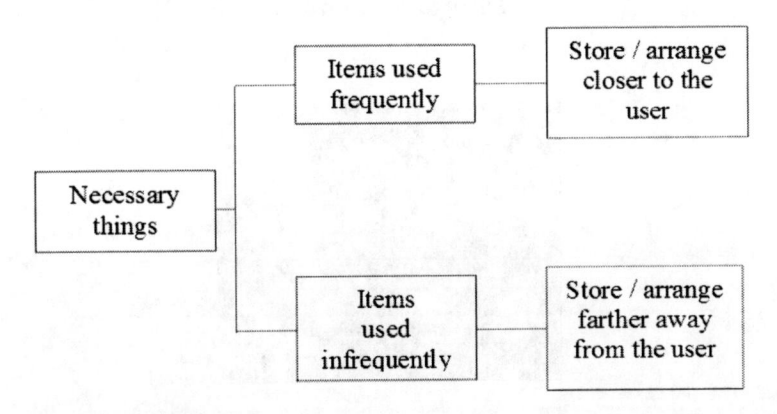

```
                        ┌─ Items used frequently ─── Store / arrange closer to the user
Necessary things ──┤
                        └─ Items used infrequently ─── Store / arrange farther away from the user
```

### i. Items used frequently

Such items are stored and arranged closer to the user because they are needed frequently. For example, in a kitchen, knives, spoons, the salt container, etc. are the items which housewives need frequently. So such items should be arranged very close to the food preparation area in the kitchen. In an office, pens, pencils, paper clips, staplers, etc. should be stored very close to the user.

*Disorganized drawer*

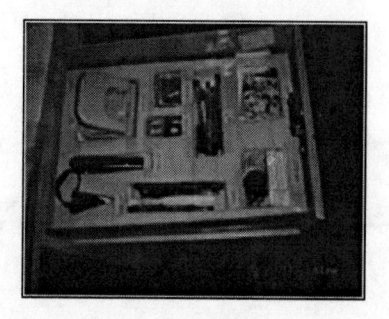

*An organized drawer*

The above two pictures show a well arranged drawer and a disorganized one. If all items are put together without planning, it is very hard to find items and takes a long time. In this picture, the drawer has been planned. First you should select which items are to be kept in the drawer. Then using a sheet of Styrofoam (polystyrene), you should cut the sheet according to the shapes of the items which are going to be kept. Then you can store each item accordingly. Now it is very easy to retrieve any item within a short time.

## ii. Items used infrequently

Items used less often can be stored farther away from the user. Closer space can be saved for the items which are used frequently.

For example, in a kitchen, the cake mixer, grinder, blender, etc. can be stored farther away. In an office, a cabinet of office supplies, correcting fluid, scissors, etc. can be kept farther away from the user.

At the end of the Seiri step, sorting all items as wanted and unwanted should have been completed. In the Seiton step, wanted items should be categorized according to the frequency of usage. Then such items should be stored as explained above.

When these items are stored, a few guidelines should be taken into consideration in order to have a successful implementation.

### 11.1. Using the "first in first out" principle

This is a very important principle in stock handling. When necessary items are consumed, items stored earliest should be consumed first and those stored later should be consumed later. This procedure minimizes the damage to stocks and wastage due to the lapsing expiry dates. On many occasions items such as stationery are wasted because of improper storage.

This kind of practice can be used at home also. All commodities brought to the home can be stored and consumed according to this principle. Then they can be utilized most productively.

## 11.2. Allocation of a specific place for each item and storing all items in their designated places

By following this procedure, the time taken to retrieve any item can be minimized because we know the specific place where each item is kept. The importance of this principle is especially true when these items are used by more than one person.

For example, if there are several members in a home, the tube of toothpaste should be kept in a common and specific place. Otherwise every member of the family has to spend more time on finding it. It is wastage of time. Such activities minimize the productivity at home. This principle applies to every item at home, office or any workplace.

This is a picture of a canteen in the officers' mess at the police station. Here, every officer has a designated cup. The name of the officer has been printed on the cup. So, all officers should hang the cup on the specific hook designated to each officer after usage. So no one needs to rearrange the cups. Each respective officer can take his own cup without any effort. Other items have also been stored using the same strategy.

*waste paper basket*

This is a picture of traditional waste paper basket / dust bin used in offices. It has been kept on a yellow circle drawn on the floor. After emptying the bin by cleaning personnel, they have to put it back in the same location. Because of the yellow circle they can identify the location easily and as a result of this practice, everyone is comfortable.

*Specific place for telephone*

This telephone is kept on the table in a specific place. It never changes. In order to keep it in the exact place, four yellow marks have been placed on the table near the four corners of the telephone as shown in the picture. So anytime the telephone should be inside the marks. Users can identify the exact location to place the telephone easily because of the marks.

*Specific place for flower pot*

The flower pot on the table also has a specific place. It should be kept on the exact place. Four yellow marks around it make it easy.

### 11.3. Label all items in order to identify easily

By labeling, everyone can identify the necessary item correctly and easily. So the probability for retrieving wrong items becomes minimal. This is a very good method for mistake-proofing. Even a person who is not familiar with the environment of the place can retrieve necessary items by reading labels and without the help of others.

Sometimes you cannot make such marks on the items or near them because of the nature of the items. The above picture shows such a situation. This shows some kind of linens used in a hospital. These have been sterilized. So only thing you can do is labelling as shown in the picture.

On most occasions, labelling can be done using colours. It can be called "visual labelling." It reduces the time taken to read written labels. At a glance any one can identify the item required.

This picture shows three sets of files but all of items are the same in appearance. When more people handle these files, they face problems in finding the exact file because they have to read all the labels. After using the file it has to be put back in the same place. But the possibility to changing the location is high when more people are involved in this task. After few days or weeks, there would be a considerable confusion and the files would have to be rearranged frequently.

In order to avoid this, a coloured cross line is drawn as shown in the picture or coloured adhesive tape can be fixed accordingly. For three shelves, different colours are used. It avoids keeping files on the wrong shelf. If a file is kept on the wrong shelf the colour mismatch shows it quickly and the cross line prevents keeping files in the wrong location. If someone keeps the file in the wrong location the continuity of the line breaks. This type of methodology saves time, stress and confusion also. A person who cannot read also can maintain this system as it is visual.

*Another file rack used same methodology*

### 11.4. Every item stored should be accessible

Storing and arranging items should be done properly so that they are easily accessible. Otherwise the probability of causing accidents may increase. Barriers to access also consume more time. It means lower productivity.

*Difficult to reach*

*Easy to reach*

## 11.5. Items used frequently should be closer to the user

Every item used frequently should be stored closer to the user. Then the usage of such items is easier and the time taken for retrieval is also less. In addition, ergonomics should be considered to minimize the body movements. It minimizes fatigue also.

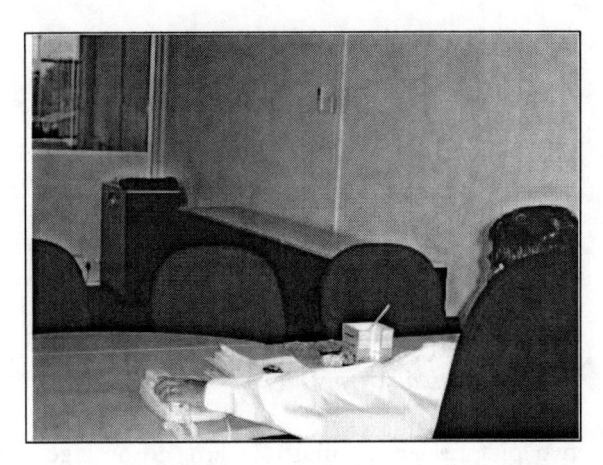

*Telephone is near to the user*

The above picture shows where to locate the telephone on the table. Normally, somebody has to answer the phone while sitting on the chair. When the telephone starts ringing the person sitting on the chair should be able to take the receiver quickly without any extra effort. The best move of the arm has been shown in the picture. The telephone has been stationed within arm's length. That is the easiest movement. If the telephone is kept farther than the arm's length, the person sitting on the chair has to bend aside. So it is an extra burden to the body and more effort has to be made to grab the phone. It is compatible with ergonomics also.

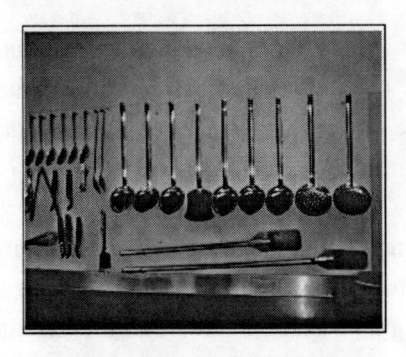

*Main items in the kitchen*

*Main items in the kitchen*

The two pictures above illustrate how to arrange a bakery kitchen. Different kinds of spoons have been located in order to be retrieved easily. The ingredient bins have also been placed accordingly.

**11.6. Minimize the retrieval time as much as possible**

Storing items improperly increases the retrieval time. Wasting time means low productivity. For example, if you don't keep the knife in a specific place in the kitchen, it takes a longer time to find it. So you spend time without result and it is wastage. Imagine how much time we spend on searching for requisites rather than on the actual task.

Likewise, calculate the time taken to retrieve necessary files in an office. Now it is understood that all these examples explained the importance of saving time because it leads to productivity improvement.

The following two pictures show the vast difference between a tool box and a tool board. If all tools are stored in a box, how long does it take to grab a specific tool? Can the exact tool be grabbed at once? Not at all. A person has to search for a long time in order to grab a tool.

Observe the second picture. All the tools have been stationed properly. Any tool can be identified at a glance. It takes only a few seconds. So you can understand how items should be arranged in order to minimize the retrieval time. Can you notice that the first wrench of the second picture is darker than others? Really it is not a wrench. It is shadow of the wrench painted in black on the board. If you remove other wrenches, you can see the same shadow marks on the board. This type of a system helps to check that all wrenches are on the board at any time especially at the end of the day. If a shadow prevails, it means that the wrench in that specific place is missing or is somewhere else. Likewise any item can be placed using shadow diagrams.

*Disorganized tool box*

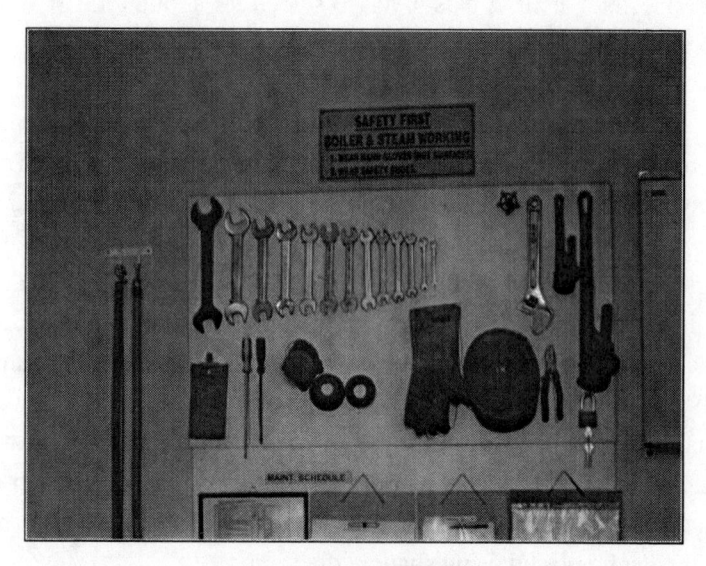

*Properly organized tools*

The following picture shows a filing cabinet. A list of files included in the drawers has been displayed on each drawer. When the list is prepared, names of files have been listed in alphabetical order. So anyone who needs a file can access it easily and retrieve the file. This type of arrangement reduces the retrieval time.

*Properly arranged filing cabinet*

*Well-planned file rack*

The above three pictures show a set up of file racks in the record room of a office. These are very valuable documents which cannot be destroyed quickly. So they have to be conserved for a reasonable time period. However, frequently files have to be retrieved. Different colours have been used to identify different racks. In addition file groups have been numbered accordingly. Such a system also reduces the stress, effort and time for retrieval.

*Railway platform in Japan*

The above picture shows the exact location where passengers have to be queued in to get on to the train. The train stops in an exact location every time in order for doors to open in front of the marks made on the platform. The lines drawn show where the doors should be aligned. So passengers queue without any interruption to others.

*Staircase in a railway station*

When the same staircase is used by passengers who are going up and coming down it creates disturbances for each other. Especially in peak times, this situation becomes worse. In order to avoid such difficulty, a line has been drawn in yellow to divide the staircase as shown in the above picture. Arrows have been drawn showing the up and down directions in each divided lane.

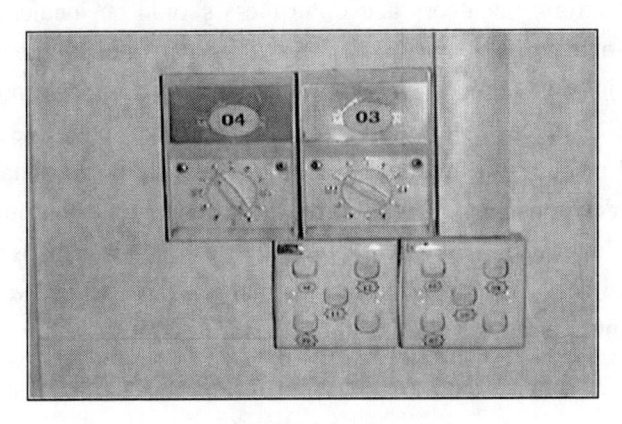

*Switches and fan controls*

When more than one switch or control has been fixed in the same place on the wall, how can you identify the exact switch to be on or off at once? Sometimes you will be able to do it after a period of time when you get used to it. How about a newcomer? Such a person cannot do that. In order to make it easy, a number is given to each switch or control as shown in the above picture. So the appropriate instrument (bulb, fan or AC) is given the number belongs to the each switch or control. Now any one can select the exact switch or control easily.

*A classroom in primary section*

Maintining neatness and orderliness should be inculcated in everyone's mind. However, it is easy to do at an early age of life especially at school. The above picture shows a class room of grade 1 students. Before introducing 5S in this school, teachers faced difficulty in guiding students to keep desks and chairs in an orderly manner. After introducing 5S, locations were marked in yellow as shown in the picture and the children were asked to station desks and chairs inside the marked cage. After two days students were able to do it right.

# CHAPTER 12

## Seiso – Cleaning / Shining

The third step of 5S is cleaning or maintaining the neatness. It is also called "shining." The set up created under step 2 has to be maintained properly and cleanly in order to obtain the maximum results of 5S implementation. Continuous removing of substances or debris which creates a dirty environment is very important.

If the working environment is neat and clean, it is easy to perform the required job. Especially machines and tools in the workplace have to be very clean. This reduces breakdowns also. It helps to detect any faults or malfunctions early. In order to maintain a clean environment, a few steps can be followed.

**12.1. Allocate 5-10 minutes for cleaning daily and encourage participation by every employee in cleaning during this time.**

*Daily cleaning*

Most organizations where 5S is implemented have allocated a few minutes in cleaning either in the morning or in the afternoon. During this period, music is also played in order to give the signal of the starting time for cleaning. During this interlude, all employees participate in cleaning the workplace, machines, tools, etc. This kind of practice encourages employees to work as a team. The ultimate result will be high morale of employees.

## 12.2. Identify a responsible person to coordinate the task in each section, department, or segment

Identification of a responsible person is very important. He or she can coordinate this activity and lead the team properly. This person should be capable to coordinate all the employees. So the selection should be done carefully. The person who is selected for this purpose should be acceptable to all other employees.

## 12.3. Inspect the workplace neatness frequently.

Regular inspection of implementation of 5S is also essential. Otherwise the enthusiasm of other members for the implementation of 5S may diminish gradually. Then the work environment may return to its former improper condition. If the management is keen on the continuation of implementation of 5S, it can be continued forever. In order to make this process successful, 5S patrol teams can be formed and these teams will be able to supervise and coordinate the implementation of 5S. These patrol teams should identify the areas to be developed and should discuss them with other employees to find the most appropriate changes to be done for the betterment of the organization.

## 12.4. Cleaning, polishing and fixing should be done continuously

Under the 5S implementation process, cleaning alone is not adequate. In order to maintain the workplace, further improvements such as polishing are required. In addition, all items should be checked to confirm whether these items are operating properly. If something has gone wrong, it has to be rectified quickly. Frequent checks help to maintain this process properly and it prevents heavy losses and damages. In addition, this practice strengthens safety.

## 12.5. Organizing big cleaning days in the workplace.

All employees in the organization get together and clean all the areas and materials on the cleaning day. All members, including top management, participate in this event. In this cleaning process, unnecessary items identified can also be sent to the red tag area. This kind of event creates team building and, as a result, every employee will have a positive feeling for his organization. That is a sense of ownership. So as they start loving their organization, they are dedicated to the organization. This type of behavior creates high morale. So this is a practical method to create high morale and to create a sense of ownership among employees.

# CHAPTER 13

## Seiketsu – Standardization

*Parking lots have been marked*

The fourth step of 5S is mostly concentrated on standardization and continuous improvement. The great challenge of the 5S system is to maintain and continue it according to the specific guidelines mentioned in the first, second and third steps. In order to facilitate this process, some kinds of standards can be set and the system can be maintained according to the standards. In addition, the members of the organization can introduce simple changes to improve the system for better results. Introducing simple positive changes helps an organization to improve its activities continuously without much effort and cost.

In step 2 (Seiton), allocating a specific place for every item was emphasized. Under step 4 (Seiketsu), all items are labeled according to the universal standards. Items which don't have universal standards can be labeled according to the local or other applicable standards.

For example, lines which transport gas, water, electricity, etc. should be painted in appropriate standard colours. Fire extinguishers should be labeled according to the standards. Such type of standardization facilitates easy identification and minimizes hazards.

A few symbols used on very common occasions are illustrated below.

*Exit*

*Emergency exit*

*No swimming*

The following guidelines will be helpful to implement Seiketsu successfully.

### 13.1. Continuation of Seiri, Seiton and Seiso and introducing new improvements to the system.

Steps have to be taken to continue Seiri, Seiton and Seiso, and meanwhile, simple and easy improvements should be introduced to the system. Then the system is improved gradually and productivity is also improved.

*Improved environment*

For example, by applying steps Seiri, Seiton and Seiso, an organization can be converted to a fascinating place. However, according to the creativity and innovativeness of the members of the organization, more improvements can be introduced. After the application of these first three steps, an organization would be very neat and proper. However, keeping flower pots, improving visitors' area, putting directions, improving work manuals, developing an evaluation system, etc. make more improvements to the system.

*Well planned and improved reception area*

In addition, access roads can be clearly indicated by drawing arrows according to the standards. Displaying slogans, messages, information and sign boards are some of the tools that can be introduced to the system.

*Tiger lines to highlight barriers*

In order to warn for danger, "tiger lines" are used. Some productivity practitioners called this type of line "zebra lines." However, I prefer to call them tiger lines because of black and yellow colours. It is a standard symbol to warn of danger. It warns to be careful near such places.

*Slogans have been displayed*

In the above picture, different kinds of slogans have been displayed in an attractive manner. This is the access road to a school. So every student can read these slogans daily and it makes a vital impact to direct students in positive path. These types of improvement do not cost much too.

*Standard symbols and signs*

This is a picture on a school's premises. Every tree has been named with its local name and botanical name. So this is another improvement introduced by students. In addition to the knowledge given in the classroom, practical knowledge can be obtained from the environment as the school environment has been improved accordingly.

*Properly marked fire points for easy identification*

*Natural composter*

This is another improvement introduced by a group of students in a school. It is a natural composter. It has been made of natural plants. It has been arranged as a cage. All organic debris is put into this cage and after a few weeks compost can be removed through a hole made at the bottom of the cage. It can be used as a perpetual composter by maintaining with minor repairs.

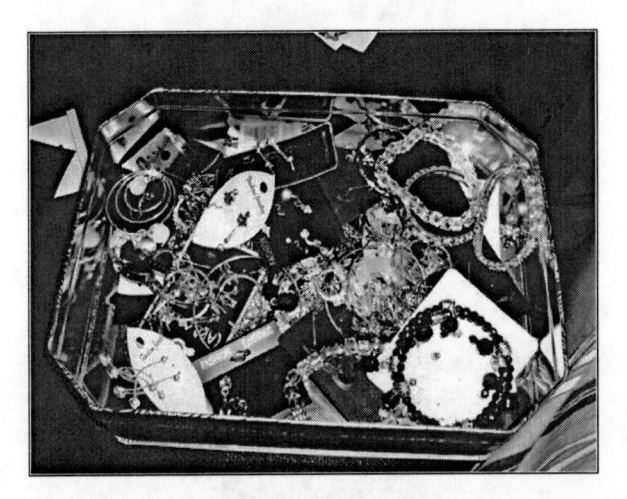

*A jewellery container*

This is a jewellery container. How long do you need to find jewellery from this box? Using simple improvements all these items can be organized neatly and it will be very easy to pick the item required. The following picture shows the way that all items have been organized on the door of a closet.

*Properly organized jewellery*

*A steel cabinet in which all the forms are in*

This picture shows a steel cabinet in which all the forms used in an office are stored. When the forms are consumed, they have to be re-ordered. In order to identify the re-order level easily, three coloured marks have been located near each form stack.

The marks are in red, yellow and green respectively. When the height of the stack is within the green range, no action is required. When the height reaches the yellow range, that type of form should be re-ordered. If it is in the red range, immediate action should be taken to get the respective form and refill. This type of mechanism makes it easy for everyone to manage their day to day activities without any shortfall.

The following few pictures explain the impact gained in an electricity distribution centre (in Sri Lanka) after introducing 5S. The electrical engineer is the in charge of that station. His main responsibility is to provide an uninterrupted electricity supply to the customers of his region. One main function that he should perform is maintaining the stocks of different items which are to be used for repairs. Every month he has to take book stocks and compare with the physical stock. Every year auditors come to have final verification. When he compares the physical stock with book figures, he has to employ at least 3-4 people for 2-3 days. During that period he is very busy and no one can contact him. It is a tiresome job for him also. A few developments made to the system after introducing 5S, eliminated his difficulties.

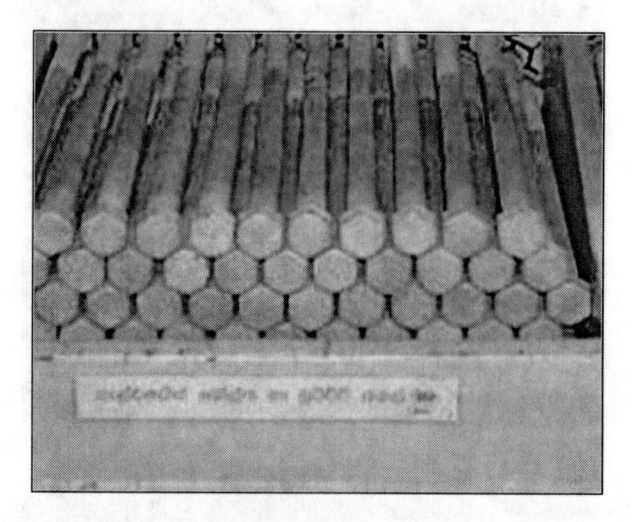

How long do you need to count these bolts to check with the book value? At least you need 5 minutes. If you can develop a system to make the count at a glance, you would be happy. The following picture shows how to do that.

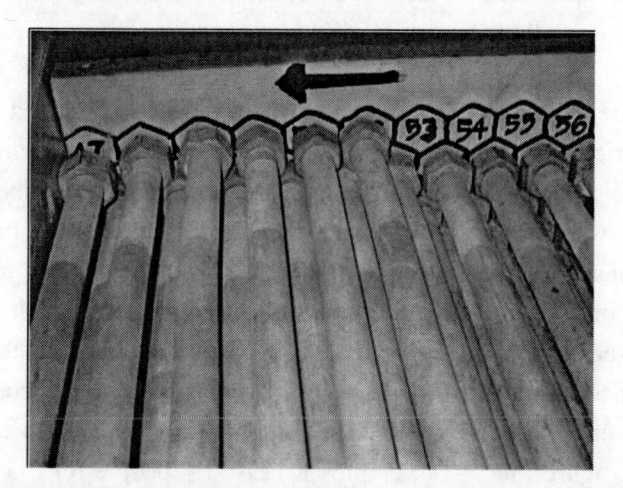

From the bottom of the container, the location of each bolt has been numbered. With an arrow, it indicates that where to start when removing the bolts out. As soon as you look at the container you can get the count of the remaining amount. It takes only few seconds.

This type of methodology can be adopted if the number of bolts is less. If it is more another developed strategy should be adopted. The following picture illustrates such a situation.

In this picture the number of bolts in each line has been marked on the white strip pasted in the box. You can clearly see it in the following picture.

When the box is full, there are 1232 bolts (616x2) in the box. So anyone can take the count of the remaining bolts easily within a few seconds.

Likewise the following pictures explain a different type of storing which you can understand easily.

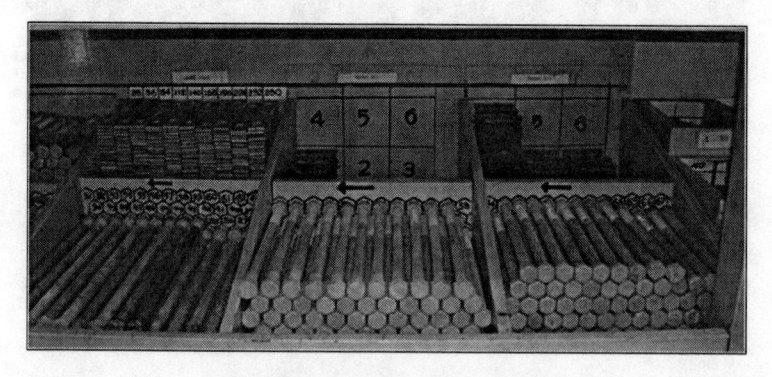

*Different kinds of bolts and plates*

*Another type of storing*

Now you can imagine how a simple thought leads to a huge change which creates a huge impact on the productivity improvement of any process. After introducing such types of changes, the electrical engineer's office became as a role model to others and the engineer is now free to do his main duties.

These types of improvements also fall under the kizen creations. If anyone can think creatively, these changes are not miracles.

## 13.2. Investigating the progress of the implementation of 5S

Under the step of Seiketsu, the progress of implementation of 5S is also reviewed and necessary changes are made according to the recommendations given by the members of the implementation group.

The commitment and dedication of the top management of the organization is essential for the success of this. They should also review the progress of the implementation of 5S and applaud positive results. They should also identify the areas to be developed further, and direct the members to focus their attention on these areas. This should be done to motivate and encourage team members rather than criticize any shortcomings. Therefore, all members can be encouraged to continue 5S and it will help to maintain a productive work environment.

**13.3. Appreciating and encouraging members involved in 5S implementation.**

Top management should appreciate the members who are involved in the 5S process and publicly praise people who show exceptional achievements. It will encourage others to join the process and it leads to 100% participation by the employees. Appreciation can be in the form of financial rewards or non-financial benefits such as training or commendation certificates, etc.

**13.4. Conducting 5S competitions between sections or divisions.**

Competitiveness is an essential feature to improve productivity everywhere. Hence, competitions increase competitiveness. Then more improvements will be introduced into the organization by workers. The winners can be rewarded. This can be done weekly, monthly, or annually and the frequency of competitions depends on the availability of funds in the organization. However all competitions should be conducted in a peaceful and friendly manner.

# CHAPTER 14

## Shitshuke- Sustaining/Discipline

The four steps discussed above alone are not adequate to stabilize productivity improvements sustainably in an organization. Without sustainable stabilization of these improvements, any organization cannot maintain the productivity levels satisfactorily and it is wastage of effort and resources also. Therefore, the fifth step is vital to keep and maintain acquired productivity levels and to move further. Not only in an organization but also in the whole society, establishing productive discipline is essential. In this step, training all the members in the organization in the implementation phase of 5S is done and all members are encouraged to implement it as a habitual activity. There are a few steps to be followed to perform this step successfully. This should be a self-motivated discipline rather than a forced program.

### 14.1. Educating others on 5S

Educating members of the organization, followers and family members on 5S should be done in order to make this concept familiar everywhere. The message about 5S can be disseminated to every citizen in the country. People who know 5S should teach it to others. Then there will be a multiplier effect. Popularizing of productivity concepts among every citizen makes productivity achievements easier and faster.

### 14.2. Keeping the workforce motivated to continue 5S

This is an essential responsibility of top management. Treating workers well and creating self-confidence is very important to keep the workforce lively and energetic. This leads to minimal conflicts between workers and the management. As a result, confidence in top management can be strengthened. It also eradicates unnecessary fear of the management among workers. If workers are under pressure and stress, the quality of the output will be minimal. It leads to low productivity.

### 14.3. Be a good listener

Being a good listener is an essential feature of leaders. In the process of implementation of 5S, most of the members are like leaders. Therefore, the ability to listen to others patiently rather than issuing orders brings more fruitful results. After listening to others, the most appropriate ideas or suggestions can be selected and they can be implemented collectively. Then everyone works happily as a team because everyone's ideas are taken into consideration. The top leadership of the organization should also abide by this requirement.

### 14.4. Follow the rules and regulations in the organization

As well as stipulating rules and regulations in an organization, obeying them is very important. This will facilitate the maintenance of the 5S process properly also. The management especially should take care of the implementation of rules and regulations impartially. Discriminatory treatment destroys the self-confidence, dedication and courage of employees. Then it is practically impossible to align workers towards the goals of the organization, which creates a negative impact on the productivity improvement of the organization. As an example, if uniforms, safety boots, safety hats, etc. have been made compulsory in the workplace, everyone should follow these procedures. Likewise, there may be so many rules and regulations enforced by each organization and those may vary from organization to organization.

### 14.5. Be punctual

This is an essential habit which has to be followed by everyone. The importance and benefits of punctuality were discussed in chapter 4. In addition, punctuality creates good discipline in an organization and it helps to utilize time productively in the work premises.

### 14.6. Keep your place neat and clean

By maintaining the workplace as well as your home properly and neatly, you can create a fascinating environment which reduces the stress in your mind. A clear mind without stress is more powerful and it leads to creativity and innovation. In addition, an attractive environment enhances the morale of the workers and it inspires them to work more productively. High morale improves the quality of the output. A workforce with high morale is one of the main assets of any organization.

Therefore, anyone who needs to improve productivity can follow these guidelines. The top management commitment is an essential and vital factor. They should also direct employees to participate in this process. With a team effort, this type of change is very easy and everyone will contribute positively. It is a proven fact that 5S is a key step to improve productivity in every organization.

**Have you heard about the sixth S?**

Some productivity practitioners explain "safety" as sixth S. However, it is not suitable to treat safety as sixth S. The 5S concept is a sequential process which has to be implemented step by step. Once all five steps are implemented properly safety prevails as a result of that. It is built-in component in the 5S concept. Hence, there is no need to discuss safety as a separate step. Where 5S is, safety is there also. In addition, security and satisfaction are also the end results of implementation of 5S. Therefore, introducing them also as additional 'S"s is not appropriate and practical as all of them ate the final outcome of application of 5S.

# CHAPTER 15

# Challenges for Implementation of 5S

Although many concepts are very good and productive, it is common to observe some barriers when such concepts are introduced into an organization. Some objections and contradictory ideas usually come up. However, implementation of productive concepts should not be set aside even though there are some barriers. Barriers or objections should be identified carefully in advance and during the implementation, and remedial action should be taken to avoid such situations wisely. Some common barriers are discussed in this chapter to have an idea in advance.

**15.1. Resistance to change**

Everyone resists change. It is a universal experience and part of human nature. People like to stay in the environment which they are used to. No one likes to change his usual chair with someone else, even when asked to do so. Likewise, no one likes to change their seat in the class, their usual style of dress, etc. because of this common characteristic. People dislike changing any habit unless the benefits of the changes are convincing.

However, new creations don't materialize without change. The world has been altered and modified because of change. Therefore, positive changes make a productive impact on day to day living. From the point of view of productivity improvement, innovations and creations are the main elements. Innovation and creations mean changes.

Most countries have developed because they introduced positive changes into their economy, infrastructure, industry, education system, health, etc. Hence, it is obvious that changes create a new world.

Therefore, managers should introduce changes in their organization and they should convince others of the positive impacts of each change. Then the employees will understand and the managers will be able to implement changes more easily. Everyone should be educated about the positive impacts and benefits before implementing 5S and productivity concepts anywhere.

## 15.2. Inability to identify own potential

Every person has a potential to think and perform any activity. Sometime it is hidden. This potential expands and multiplies when a person is exposed to education, awareness and when he gains practical experience. However, some people are reluctant to face challenges. Commonly people start questioning their ability to make the changes or their ability to understand the methods to do so. Negative and backward thinking may start to dominate. The reason is that such persons cannot identify their potential.

However, more education and awareness strengthen the ability to identify potential and also it helps to increase the potential. As a result of that, a person becomes highly confident. Confidence is the main key to any type of success. It opens doors to innovative thinking. Innovative thinking adds more creations to the world in different forms. The awareness and implementation of 5S can be considered as a powerful tool to enhance potential. It leads to breakaways. The people with more potential start releasing it in different ways. (Sometimes it may be released in a harmful way to the society.) By directing people towards positive behaviours, harmful outputs can be eliminated.

The following pictures give some examples of releasing individual potential.

*A group of students in a school released their potential*

*The Wright brothers released their potential*

*Leonardo da Vinci released his potential*

*Group of engineers released their potential (Victoria Reservoir-Sri Lanka)*

*Mughal emperor Shah Jahan released his potential*

Likewise this world has been developed because of different kinds of potential in different people. What type of potential do you have? Can you add something fruitful to the global community?

### 15.3. Misconception of "I am always right; others are not."

Some people used to think, "I am always right; others are not." and that they are more knowledgeable than others. This may cause damage to the smooth running of any organization. Other members of the organization may also have different kinds of knowledge which managers don't have, and that can be more useful to the organization. Thus, the best idea is to encourage a collective effort to achieve the goals of the organization. Therefore, leaders and top management should listen to others and take their ideas into consideration when new changes are introduced. The ability to listen to others is an invaluable quality of leaders.

### 15.4. Reluctance to listen to subordinates

Some people are reluctant to listen to their subordinates because of their status, designation, age, etc. This may block the opportunity to have valuable and productive ideas from their subordinates. This will be harmful to the implementation of 5S because implementation of 5S is based on team effort. Hence, it is important to listen to good suggestions which also come from subordinates. It is the best way of receiving a large number of good suggestions from suggestion schemes, which were discussed earlier in this book.

### 15.5. Mental stress

When there is considerable mental stress, it is impossible to have a calm mind. If you don't have a calm mind it is impossible to plan any activity and implement it properly. Due to mental stress, most people try to procrastinate or postpone daily activities and they think they will perform them after the stress is diminished. This never happens because delayed work increases stress further.

Creating an attractive, well-planned environment and a good work set-up make a substantial contribution to minimize the mental stress. 5S is the appropriate method to create an easy-going working environment. So, creating a sound working environment by implementing 5S is much more fruitful than spending time with frustration.

## 15.6. Old traditional negative attitudes and habits

Some people don't like to change old and traditional habits and try to stick to them even though they understand the positive impacts of new changes. This is because of a dislike of anything "out of the box." Such people also act as barriers to changes. This situation becomes worse and dangerous when top management has such qualities, because new dynamic changes cannot be introduced due to their resistance. Every member of the management team should be educated about new knowledge and technology, and they should be updated continuously. This leads to minimization of the resistance created from such people due to old attitudes.

## 15.7. Over-estimation

Some managers over-estimate their organizations although the organization needs more changes to bring the organization to a more productive level. They never introduce new changes due to their over-estimation. It is an unfortunate situation because they cannot achieve targets even within their capacity. The management of other organizations, who studies current management developments and changes and applies them into their organizations, serves such organizations as excellent models. Hence, benchmarking other organizations and observing best practices is more fruitful rather than continuation of over-estimation. The 5S concept is a good remedy to eradicate such misconceptions.

## 15.8. Lack of communication between employees and management

Before implementing or introducing 5S, all employees should be informed about the new plan and its advantages. Otherwise employees get confused or shocked. They may think this new plan is another way of getting profits by labour exploitation and hard working. If it happens there may be rumours which adversely affect the expected outcome. Hence, the team or management should educate employees well on the positive outcome and the benefits of such implementation.

# CHAPTER 16

## Application of 5S Concept to your Mind

*Environment refreshes your mind*

The methodology of applying the 5S concept in any place including offices, home, schools, etc., was discussed in earlier chapters. However, the most important application of 5S is to apply it to your mind. It should be done first even before it is introduced anywhere else. By applying 5S into the mind, step by step, anyone can have a good mind. This leads to success in every activity. This is the way of setting your mind productively. Therefore, let's consider the way to apply the 5S concept to the mind.

### 16.1. Application of Seiri

First you have to identify necessary and unnecessary thoughts in your mind and remove unwanted (unnecessary) or unproductive thoughts immediately. Anger, jealousy, and hate, are some of the characteristics/traits which create bad and harmful thoughts. Such traits should be removed by controlling the mind. Spending time to criticize others and to find others' mistakes and faults means wasting your own valuable time which could be used to make your life more productive. It opens paths to degradation or collapse in your life.

You have to retain and maintain only good thoughts in your mind and always you should try to keep your mind clean. Then you will be able to control your mind wisely.

### 16.2. Application of Seiton

After the application of Seiri, only good thoughts remain in your mind. Now you can plan your future successfully. After identification of the things you have to do, you have to prioritize them according to their importance. The most important activity or step should be initiated first. Likewise, you can set targets for each activity which you have identified and set priorities. Next, you have to think and find strategies to achieve the targets and get the expected results. It would be the action plan for your life.

However, the priorities vary according to age, culture, personality, style, etc, and anyone can identify his or her own priorities to achieve a successful life. For example, a person who is still a child has to give priority for his studies and career development activities which build up the personality and self confidence. If he has a clear mind with good thoughts, it is very easy to concentrate the mind on the activities which make your future successful. The childhood is the best stage to inculcate good thoughts and it is the turning point which creates the whole foundation of his future. Orientations of children for teamwork such as playing, camping, volunteering and charitable activities are some of very easy steps to initiate building up a person in the childhood. Such types of activities create good qualities such as helping others, sharing with others and respecting others. Most developed countries encourage such activities. In some provinces in Canada, each student who hopes to graduate in high school must complete a minimum number of volunteer hours (Ontario – 40 hours) and it is compulsory. Such types of activities create good qualities in their minds. When children are involved in such activities, they never get any opportunities to focus their mind on any bad type of things or to involve in such activities. If the mind is concentrated on wrong activities in childhood, life would not be successful. The people who are physically, emotionally and spiritually strong will be a great asset of any nation. Therefore, the application of Seiton creates a good plan for life and sets the path for success.

### 16.3. Application of Seiso

The normal environment gets dirty frequently by dust and other particles. Likewise, the mind is also polluted by negative thoughts frequently. Even though the mind is cleared as explained in 16.2, polluting it daily is natural. However, you should be able to set barriers for the upcoming negative thoughts. No outsider can do this for you. Once a thought is created in your mind, you instantly have to identify whether it is positive or negative. If it is negative, you should remove or eradicate it quickly by controlling your mind. You are the most powerful person for controlling your mind. If you need, you can.

If your mind is full of negative thoughts, it minimizes the room for creating positive thoughts. If your mind is full of positive thoughts, the room for negative thoughts is minimal. So you should always try to keep your mind full of positive thoughts. Hence, you should be able to create defensive mental barriers for negative thoughts.

When you identify a thought as a negative one, try to evaluate and estimate the damage which could be caused if it prevails in your mind. Then you can realize the damage. So you can remove such thoughts from your mind immediately.

If your mind is full of positive thoughts your responses and actions will also be positive. If your mind is full of negative thoughts your actions will also be negative and they will be definitely harmful to you as well as others. Then you will not be able to sleep well, eat well or perform any activity happily.

Having cleansed your mind as explained, you can gradually strengthen your mind with positive thoughts and finally you will have a very strong mind.

## 16.4. Application of Seiketsu

Always it is necessary to apply Seiri, Seiton, and Seiso into your mind in order to maintain a refreshed mind. In addition, you should always try to create more positive thoughts in your mind. It helps to strengthen the mind. This is also a continuous improvement process of your mind.

For example, reading good books, helping others, giving your knowledge to others, and social service activities are some steps that can be carried out to improve your mind. In addition, meditation is the strongest powerful method of positive streamlining of your mind. By doing so, you can get self-satisfaction. Self-satisfaction leads to a positive mind.

In addition, you can imagine and do more innovative things which benefit you as well as society. People who have fresh minds can create more innovative ideas which may create great changes in the world. Such persons don't have time to pinpoint others' mistakes or to do harmful things to others. Their minds are always full of good and productive thoughts. Hence, their physical health will also be better and better.

### 16.5. Application of Shitsuke

After application of the first four steps, such a person becomes great. So his mentality is rich and full of good ideas. Under this step, he has to teach his experiences and share his knowledge with others and attract others to follow him or his great achievements.

All religious leaders did this and they were able to enlighten their minds and they preached their findings to human society. However, it is not easy to control your mind like religious leaders such as Lord Buddha, Jesus Christ, or Mohammed. But you can achieve a tremendous amount if you have the need and commitment. In order to make it easier, you should have a clear knowledge of the way your mind works.

According to the nature of thoughts, thoughts create feelings. Good thoughts create good feelings and bad thoughts create bad feelings. According to the nature of feelings, your behaviour varies. If feelings are good, your behaviour and actions will be good. If feelings are bad, your behaviour and actions will be bad.

"Thoughts" mean some ideas generated in your brain and "feelings" are senses which are based on the thoughts created in the brain. For example, if you have a need to read a newspaper, a thought comes from the brain first. So, the necessity to read the newspaper is a thought. Generating a necessity to have food is also a thought. As soon as thoughts generate in your mind, feelings also come with them. These cannot be separated. Happiness, sadness, pain, anger, love, and kindness are some of feelings generated in your mind.

We cannot observe or see thoughts externally. Feelings also cannot be observed externally. However, the behaviour which these thoughts and feelings inspire can be observed externally. It means that anyone can understand the way of your thinking by observing your behaviour.

So, good thinking creates good thoughts. Good thoughts create good feelings. Good feelings lead to good behaviour. If you can have good thinking, it can be called productive thinking. A mind without productive thinking decreases productivity. Perhaps it leads to destruction of property as well as life.

It is clear that feelings create a strong impact on the lifestyle. Death may occur due to the uncontrollable feelings such as extreme envy, sadness, anger, extreme loneliness, etc. People cannot bear these feelings and as a result quick damages including death can occur.

However, the application of 5S helps to control your feelings well because it is a strategic method to arrange your mind properly. If you have a clear and calm mind, you will be able to gradually release stress caused by extreme feelings. If you try to release your feelings at once, such a situation cannot be borne and damage occurs.

Therefore, let's discuss some common ways of releasing stress gradually without any harmful impact.

### 16.6. Ways of releasing stress

### 16.6.1 Releasing sounds like crying or shouting

By releasing sounds, stress can be minimized. When you feel sad you tend to cry or shout and it is a natural way of releasing the sadness gradually. Even when you have a physical pain; the nervous system automatically starts releasing sound in different forms such as crying, screaming, moaning, etc. It also helps to reduce the pain.

### 16.6.2. Telling the story to others

If you can tell the facts that create stress to others, it helps to reduce your mental pain or stress and so releases the mental burden to some extent. So, you feel relief after you tell your story to others who can listen to you and give some positive comments and advice to you. Hence, it is better to share your stressful feelings with your best friends, teachers, or parents, etc. There is a famous saying: "A trouble shared is a trouble halved."

### 16.6.3. Resting and relaxing

When you have a stressful mind, it is better to rest and find some time for relaxation. So you can change your environment and have a rest. Then your stress starts decreasing gradually and it will help you to think calmly and it is the way to find the best solutions for the problems which increased your stress.

### 16.6.4. Sleeping for a specific period.

Sleep is also a good remedy to reduce stress in your mind. After a good and comfortable sleep, your mind will be more fresh and calm than before you went to sleep. Sleeping means good rest. A rested mind is also more apt to be able to find solutions to the problems that caused the stress.

### 16.6.5. Listening to music

Music is a very good medication for a stressful mind. It can reduce stress substantially. So if you can listen to music or sing a song which you prefer, your stress reduces drastically. In addition, it helps to divert your mind away from the causes of the stress to another direction.

In addition to these remedies, you can read a good book, go sightseeing, or change the stressful environment in order to reduce the stress. If you are comfortable, meditation is another strong remedy to reduce stress. So, it is understood that there are so many options to reduce and relax your stress which may be harmful to your body and the life. It has been proven that physical exercise also helps to reduce stress it helps you prepare for better and more productive sleep.

Having implemented such remedies, your mind will be very powerful and you will feel that there is nothing which cannot be done. It means that every challenge can be overcome. At the beginning of a challenge, you might feel that it cannot be met and no solutions can be found. However, you can improve your mind and then you will be able to succeed in anything. It is self-confidence. If you have good self-confidence, you can achieve everything in the world. People who changed the world had very strong minds and self-confidence. Scientists, philosophers, architects, inventors, etc, are the people who introduce innovations to the world. Innovations are not easy but with self-confidence, it becomes easier. A person with a clear mind can have a clean environment. His body is also clean. His office, home and whole environment become clean. If everybody's mind could be cleansed, the whole world would be clean and interesting. That's why the application of 5S into the mind is encouraged. It leads to a high quality and productive lifestyle. It means happiness.

What is happiness? According to Buddhism, happiness is the greatest wealth in the world. Any wealth, including money, without happiness doesn't make any sense in your life. According to Christianity, "loving your neighbors" is taught. What does it mean? It means to love others. In order to love others, you should have a kind, calm and clear mind. Only such people can love others. People with unkind, chaotic minds cannot love others because positive thoughts never generate in their minds. That's why Jesus Christ asked his followers to love others. If all human beings could love each other, imagine the end result. How beautiful would the world be? It is happiness, harmony and peace. Without happiness, peace and harmony, no one can get the satisfaction from his life.

Hence, the application of 5S is not only a physical strategy but also it is a spiritual remedial strategy. It was highlighted by all religious leaders thousands of years ago for the betterment of human beings. 5S can be introduced as a victorious concept for success in life.

**\* Note**

I would like to include some religious beliefs stated by world famous religious leaders about the life. These will help you to have a good idea and to make your life successful. (source:- http://www.edminterfaithcentre.ca/goldrule.htm )

### Universality of the Golden Rule

"We have committed the Golden Rule to memory; let us now commit it to life."

*Edwin Markham*

### Religious Beliefs Governing Behavior toward Other People

Faith groups differ greatly in their concepts of deity, other beliefs and practices. But there is near unanimity of opinion among the world's various historical religions on how one person should treat another. Almost all religions have passages in their holy texts, or writings of their leaders, which promote the **Ethic of Reciprocity** or the **Golden Rule**.

### Baha'i Faith

"Lay not on any soul a load that you would not wish to be laid upon you, and desire not for anyone the things you would not desire for yourself."

"Ascribe not to any soul that which thou wouldst not have ascribed to thee, and say not that which thou doest not." "Blessed is he who preferreth his brother before himself." (Baha'u'llah, Gleanings, LXVI:8 )

## Brahmanism

"This is the sum of duty: do naught unto others which would cause you pain if done to you." (Mahabharata 5:1517)

## Buddhism

"Hurt not others in ways that your, yourself would find hurtful." (Udana-Varga 5.18)

"A state that is not pleasing or delightful to me, how could I inflict that upon another?" (Samyutta Nikaya v. 353)

## Christianity

"Do unto others as you would have them do unto you." (Matthew 7:12)

"...and do not do what you hate..." (Gospel of Thomas 6)

## Confucianism

"Surely it is the maxim of loving-kindness: Do not do to others what you would not have them do to you." (Analects 15:23)

"Tse-kung asked, 'Is there one word that can serve as a principle of conduct for life?' Confucius replied, 'It is the word 'shu' — reciprocity. Do not impose on others what you yourself do not desire.'" (Doctrine of the Mean 13.3)

## Hinduism

"Do not do to others what would cause pain if done to you." (Mahabharata 5.1517)

"One should not behave towards others in a way which is disagreeable to oneself." (Mencius Vii.A.4)

## Islam

"Not one of you is a believer until you wish for others what you wish for yourself." (Fourth Hadith of an-Nawawi 13)

"No one of you is a believer until he desires for his brother that which he desires for himself." (Sunnah)

## Jainism

"One should treat all creatures in the world as one would like to be treated." (Mahavira, Sutrakritamga)

"Therefore, neither does he [, a sage,] cause violence to others nor does he make others do so." (Acarangasutra 5.101-2)

"In happiness and suffering, in joy and grief, we should regard all creatures as we regard our own self." (Lord Mahavira, 24th Tirthankara)

## Training and Consultancy on Productivity Improvement – Worldwide

in
Public Sector
Private Sector
School Sector
&
Community Level
By
**Upali Marasinghe**

(Asian Productivity Organization(APO) Award Winner on Productivity Dissemination.)

**Training topics**

- 5S (Housekeeping)
- Kaizen & Innovation
- Quality Circles
- Balance Scorecard
- Work Study and Work measurement
- Deming's 14 Points on management…

Contacts- upalima2002@yahoo.co.uk

> I would like to have your views on this book and suggestions are also welcome. Write to ; upalima2002@yahoo.co.uk